TRIUMPH
OUT OF TRAGEDY
—Turning Obstacles into Opportunities

W0006428

And Other Messages

by

Ralph and Arlene Woodrow

International Standard Book Number: 0-916938-15-8

CONTENTS

1. TRIUMPH OUT OF TRAGEDY 1

2. LOOKING FORWARD 11

3. POWER GREATER THAN THE PROBLEM ... 22

4. TRIUMPHANT PRAYER 29

5. "7-UP" 38

6. TATTLERS AND BUSYBODIES 51

7. EXCUSES! 61

8. DIVINE LOVE 75

9. FREEDOM FROM FEAR 86

10. F.L.A.M.E. 93

11. "SIRS, WE WOULD SEE JESUS" 111

12. GOING HOME ANOTHER WAY 123

Chapter 1

TRIUMPH OUT OF TRAGEDY

TURNING OBSTACLES INTO OPPORTUNITIES

There is a unique monument in Enterprise, Alabama—the only monument in the world that was built to honor a pest! Unveiled in 1919, these words are inscribed on the monument: "In profound appreciation of the Boll Weevil and what it has done as the herald of prosperity, this monument was erected by the citizens of Enterprise, Coffee County, Alabama."

The boll weevil, having invaded southern Texas from Mexico in 1892, soon spread to other areas of the south. By the late summer of 1915, in Coffee County and southeast Alabama, the cotton crops had been devastated by this pest as it made its "home" in the cotton bolls.

The devastation caused by the boll weevil even found its way into a comical folk song. I can recall as a boy hearing Tex Ritter sing *The Boll Weevil Song* on the radio:

The Boll Weevil Song

De boll weevil am a little black bug, come from Mexico dey say,
Come all the way to Texas, looking for a place to stay.
He's lookin' for a home—lookin' for a home.

First time I see dee boll weevil, he was sittin' on the square;
Next I see dee boll weevil, all of his family there.
He's lookin' for a home—lookin' for a home.

Now the farmer taken the weevil, put him in the red hot sand.
Weevil say, "This is mighty hot, but I'll stand it like a man.
It'll be my home—it'll be my home."

Well the farmer take the weevil, and put him in a lump of ice.
Weevil say to the farmer, "Mighty cool and nice.
This'll be my home—this'll be my home."

Aye the farmer take the weevil and put him in dee red hot fire.
Weevil say to the farmer, "Here I are, here I are.
This'll be my home—gotta have a home."

Well the captain say to the missiz, "What do you think of dat?
The boll weevil done made a nest in my best Sunday hat!"
Gotta have a home—gotta have a home.

The merchant got half dee cotton, the boll weevil got dee rest.
Didn't leave the farmer's wife but one ole cotton dress.
It's full of holes—plum full of holes!

The farmer say to the merchant, "We's in an awful fix.
Weevil got all the cotton, left us only the sticks.
We's got no home—no sign of a home."

So why would this notorious weevil be honored by the people of Enterprise, Alabama? The answer is quite simple: it forced them to turn *tragedy into triumph!*

Confronted with the loss of their cotton harvest and facing bankruptcy, the farmers knew something had to be done. They discovered there was another crop they could grow that would be unaffected by the boll weevil: *peanuts!* Whereas every condition had to be ideal to make a living raising cotton—a cotton crop was poor seven out of ten years—being forced to raise peanuts brought a consistent prosperity to the entire area. Even a president of the United States, Jimmy Carter, came from those ranks of prosperous peanut farmers.

What is it that bugs you? It may be circumstances you are facing, things you do not understand. It may be an unreasonable boss you work for, it may be a pesky relative or neighbor. But whatever it is, God can turn it around. A blessing can come out of seeming defeat.

It has been said that when the Lord wishes to give us something special, he does not wrap it up in a glamorous package and hand it to us on a silver platter. Instead, he may bury it in a great big tough problem while he watches with anticipation to see if we have what it takes to break the problem apart and find the pearl of great price. Realizing this, instead of being defeated by an obstacle, we can ask: "What *opportunity* is here?" This simple change in attitude can throw open the floodgates of victory, for according to your faith it will be done (Matt. 9:29).

We might call this the boomerang technique. By God's help you can turn it around. You can find ways to turn a problem to your advantage. Even that which is "evil" can be turned around for "good" (Gen. 50:20). Instead of becoming *bitter*, you can become *better*. You can make lemonade out of life's sour lemons. You can turn stumbling stones into stepping stones. You can turn "NO" around so it becomes "ON." You can do it! Remember the last four letters in "American" are: I CAN. "I can do all things through Christ who strengthens me" (Phil. 4:13). "For it is God who works in you both to will and to do of his good pleasure" (Phil. 2:13). "Greater is he that is in you, than he that is in the world" (1 John 4:4).

So you have problems to deal with? *Good!* This proves you are still alive! Those without any problems are in the cemetery.

3

Often we do not understand problems. We do not understand why bad things happen to good people. We may question the well-known verse that says: "All things work together for GOOD to them that love God" (Rom. 8:28). But notice this verse does not say that each thing *individually* that happens to us is good. Admittedly, some things are bad! BUT, in God's hands, all things *"work together* for good."

A recipe may call for ingredients that would be distasteful and intolerable if taken *alone*—things like flour, vinegar, pepper, baking powder, vanilla extract,

shortening, raw eggs, and cream of tartar! But when these are "worked together" and baked in an oven, these seemingly undesirable ingredients become a mouth-watering delicacy.

So it is when the Master Chef takes the ingredients of our lives—the bitter, the bland—and blends them together. Part of the process may involve an "oven" experience for a time, but the final result will be GOOD. Once we realize this—once we believe this—once it becomes a part of us—our whole outlook changes for the better! With Paul we can say: "Thanks be unto God, who *always* causes us to triumph in Christ"! (2 Cor. 2:14).

4

Many years ago a pastor told me a humorous story of two men who went on a hunting trip. When the trip was over, all they had managed to shoot was a deer and an owl! "I guess we better cut the deer in two; you take half and I'll take half," the one man said. The other replied: "There is no need to cut the deer in two. I'll take the deer and *you* take  the owl, or *you* take the owl and I'll take the deer"! In other words, in either case the one man would get the deer, not the owl!

This would be like tossing a coin and saying: "Heads I win, tails you lose"! In each of these cases, one person would win either way; the other would lose either way.

We may have called for "heads" in life, but the coin came up "tails." But in Christ we win even when it seems we lose. Jesus said: "He that finds his life shall lose it: and he that loses his life for my sake shall find it" (Mt. 10:39). Paul wrote: "I have suffered the loss of all things...that I may win Christ" (Ph. 3:8). Though he was a loser, he was a *winner!*

Disappointments can be God's appointments, as he turns tragedy into triumph in our lives!

What is a failure: it's only a spur
To the one who receives it right.
It makes the spirit within him stir
To go in once more and fight.
If you have never failed, it's an easy guess
You have never won any high success!
—Edmond VanCooke

"Under the circumstances I can't expect success," some may say. Circumstances? Roosevelt could have hidden

5

behind his lifeless legs; Truman could have used "no college education"; and Eisenhower could have ducked behind his heart attack.

One person faces circumstances and has PEACE; another goes to PIECES. One man builds CASTLES; another digs CAVES. One man's WEED is another man's FLOWER. One man's TRASH is another man's TREASURE. It all has to do with *attitude*. The secret of success lies in what people do when they are BROKEN—not in how many BREAKS they get.

The one time the word "success" appears in the Bible (KJV), it is within a promise to Joshua while facing all kinds of adverse circumstances. Moses had died. He must now face the Amorites, Hittites, Canaanites, and Perizzites. But the divine word was that God would grant "good success" (Josh. 1:8), in spite of circumstances.

Visualize a wooden crate. Let's call it "circumstances." This crate can either confine or lift up, depending on what we do with it. It will confine us if we get under it— causing us to be blinded, burdened down, and unable to function. In this situation we are under the circumstances! But, if we take this crate called "circumstances" and position it with the solid side up, it becomes a stair step whereby we can reach higher and have a better perspective. In this way, we can be above the circumstances!

When Jesus passed through Jericho, Zacchaeus, because he was a short man, was unable to see Jesus. There were too many people in the way. He could have talked of the circumstances and been defeated. But instead of accepting failure in the matter, he did something about it. Running ahead, he climbed up into a tree. This was a simple act, but in this way he rose above the circumstances. He not only saw Jesus, but Jesus saw him and salvation came to his house.

I well recall a little song we were taught as children about Zacchaeus:

...he climbed up into a sycamore tree,
for the Lord he wanted to see.
And as the Savior passed that way,
he looked up in the tree and said:
"Zacchaeus, come down!
I'm going to your house today."

Perhaps we have failed to see Jesus because there are too many things between us and Him. Instead of "looking unto Jesus the author and finisher of our faith" (Heb. 12:1,2), it is easy to get our eyes on the tragedy, the problem, the circumstances, or people.

You may not like your present job. You may have bogged down. But this job may be the very thing that can launch you on to better things. It is like a man climbing a ladder. He may not like the level he is presently on, but it takes this step to go higher. Don't despise the present position, but begin to do the very best you can where you now are. Do it with your might (Ecc. 9:10). By making the best of it, the very thing that presently seems frustrating can be that which helps you go higher!

One man had a job answering letters in the complaint department of a large company. He became bored with his job, stumbled through it, always a week or so behind in his letter writing. But realizing his job was a valid step in the ladder, he took on a different attitude. He got caught up on his work. He composed new and better letters. Mail was answered the day it came in and answered well. His changed attitude turned him overnight from a weakling into a dynamic realist. He became a new man  moving in a new world. Soon he moved up in the company to a more fulfilling position and salary. He used the old job to get into something better.

Those who are familiar with the action of a rock tumbler, know that even rough rocks in time become smooth from constantly hitting against other rocks and take on a jewel-like appearance. So is it in life: frictions between individuals or hardships can smooth us out and make us beautiful before the Lord. We are jewels in the making (Mal. 3:17)—being polished by the Lord in the rock tumbler of life!

On a number of occasions we have been in Death Valley, California, the *lowest* spot in the United States— 282 feet below sea level. In sheer contrast, not too far distant is the *highest* elevation in the United States (except Alaska)—Mount Whitney, reaching a dizzying height of 14,495 feet. Clearly, if there were no valleys, there could be no mountain tops! Even so in life, we are able to savor the thrill of mountain top experiences because of the valleys we pass through.

It is wonderful to know Jesus Christ as our Savior. But we could never know him as our SAVIOR if we had not been SINNERS. We could not be SAVED if we were never LOST. We could not be HEALED if we were never SICK. We appreciate the DAWN because there has been a NIGHT. We do not know VICTORY unless we have known DEFEAT. Experiencing POVERTY makes us appreciate PROSPERITY.

Bitter cold weather makes us thankful for the warm sunshine. It takes a black night to reveal the splendor of the stars. Without weeds and worthless ground, we would seldom notice lovely flowers and plants. It takes war to enjoy peace, failure to enjoy success, poor crops to rejoice over an abundant harvest, hunger to enjoy food, tiredness to appreciate rest. Gold is purified because of the fire. Flowers, when crushed, bring forth their fragrance.

When we think of times of testing and trial, we remember the story of Job. Job had been a prosperous business man. But he suffered the loss of his cattle, children, wealth and health. He suffered with boils and the distress of a nagging wife. When Job could no longer lean on riches, family, or friends, he had to trust fully in the Lord. In times like this—when there is no other way to turn—our approach to God becomes positive and determined. Answers come that would otherwise be unknown.

It was during the time of Job's trial he received a determination he had not known before. "Though he slay me, yet will I trust in him," he affirmed (Job 13:15). It was during this time he received revelations about the resurrection: "For I KNOW that my redeemer liveth," he said, "and that he shall stand at the latter day upon the earth: and though after my skin worms destroy this body, yet in my flesh shall I see God" (Job 19:25-27). A greater faith, a greater determination, a greater triumph resulted from what seemed to be tragedy.

God brought Job forth "as gold" and "blessed the latter end of Job more than his beginning." His property was restored and children were born to him. His daughters were the most beautiful women in all the land. One he named Jemima. If her sister had a child, she could have been called "Aunt Jemima"!

Joseph may have thought his life was a failure when he was treated unfairly by his jealous brothers, was sold into slavery and ended up in an Egyptian prison. But there was a purpose for being in Egypt. Ultimately tragedy was turned to triumph and Joseph became a ruler of Egypt. Through being in this position, he was later able to save his whole family from being destroyed by famine.

It seemed like tragedy when Paul and Silas were thrown into jail at Philippi. But there they converted a jailer who became a key man for the establishment of the gospel in that city. Later, one of the great books of our New Testament—Philippians—was written to the church that was established as a result.

9

The tragedy of persecution actually resulted in the spread of the gospel in the early days of the church. "At that time there was a great persecution against the church...they that were scattered abroad went every where preaching the word" (Acts 8:1-4).

Finally, the greatest example of tragedy turned to triumph is at the very heart of the gospel: *the death of Jesus Christ.* Public opinion had turned against him. He who came to bring LIFE was condemned to DEATH. As He hung lifeless upon the cross, Satan could have said: "At last I have won a great victory. The gospel is a failure. Jesus is dead!" But what seemed to be Satan's greatest victory was actually the very thing which forever defeated Satan and sin.

Out of tragedy came triumph, for it did not end at the cross. Jesus rose again in victory over sin and death. Because he lives, we have life and that more abundantly. Because he lives "death is swallowed up in victory" (1 Cor. 15:55-57). Through his death and resurrection our sins are forgiven—tragedy is turned to triumph—and we stand before God with the righteousness of Christ (2 Cor. 5:21). We are complete in Him who is the head of all principality and power, "having spoiled principalities and powers, he made a show of them openly, triumphing over them in it" (Col. 2:10,15).

"God moves in mysterious ways his wonders to perform; he plants his footprints on the sea and rides upon the storm," said a poet. A prophet said that God's ways are higher than our ways—as high as the heavens are above the earth (Is. 55:9). An apostle put it this way: "O the depth of the riches both of the wisdom and knowledge of God! how unsearchable are his judgments, and his ways past finding out!" (Rom. 11:33). But regardless of how we phrase it, there is abundant evidence that God's plan for man is to turn TRAGEDY to TRIUMPH!

Chapter 2

LOOKING FORWARD

—by Ralph Woodrow

We have all faced situations that were difficult. But the stress of any present difficulty can be greatly reduced, if we look beyond this difficulty, *looking forward* to something that brings us joy.

Perhaps the greatest example of this may be seen in the life of Jesus as he faced the agony of the cross. As he prayed in the garden, he sweat as it were great drops of blood. He felt the trauma, the anguish, the torment, as he faced that crisis hour. Yet,

> "FOR THE JOY THAT WAS SET BEFORE HIM, he endured the cross, despising the shame, and is set down at the right hand of the throne of God" (Heb. 12:2).

As unpleasant as something may be, if we have something pleasant to look forward to, it stimulates hope. It is not pleasant for a person to undergo a serious surgery, yet if this is the door to life and health, such can be endured because of the good outcome.

A similar situation faces a woman who gives birth to a baby. The actual delivery may be a painful and dreaded experience. "A woman when she is in travail hath sorrow, because her hour is come: but as soon as she is delivered of the child, she remembers no more the anguish, for joy that a man is born into the world" (John 16:21). The anticipation of that joy to come, can help her through the difficult time.

One man always experienced anxiety when going to a dentist. It had become a phobia with him. In his mind, he reasoned that it was for his own good to take proper care of his teeth. This helped some. But the way he dealt more specifically with his problem was this: On the morning of his appointment, he purposely planned something for *right after his appointment* that he *liked* to do. If the appointment was from 10 until 11 in the morning, looking forward to what he was going to do *after* 11, helped him project his thoughts to the "joy set before him," rather than the unpleasantness prior to 11.

Each of us may use the same principle regarding things that bother us—by looking forward and beyond those things. This is, after all, the very basis of what "faith" is all about: "Now faith is the substance of things hoped for, the evidence of things not seen" (Heb. 11:1).

Though a man may be in prison, if he knows he will get out at a certain time, he looks forward to his freedom. He has hope! But the prisoner who has no possibility of release does not have this hope.

Things may be tough right now, but if we know the Lord, we can experience hope in knowing that *he will see us through*. As a hymn says,

Some through the water, some through the flood,
Some through the fire, but all through the blood;
Some through great sorrow, but God gives a song;
In the night season and all the day long.

The oft-quoted Twenty-third Psalm speaks of walking *"through* the valley of the shadow of death." God will take us *through;* he does not leave us there!

A man who was enduring a serious time of testing, put his finger on a Bible verse that says, "It came to pass..." By faith he applied this verse to his own situation: that this testing time did not come to *stay,* it came to *pass!* Better things were ahead.

The fact that these present difficulties will pass provides the basis of a lovely song,

These things shall pass and some great morning,
We'll look back and smile at heartaches we have known.
So don't forget when shadows gather,
The Lord our God is still the king upon his throne.

A rose looks grey at midnight, but the flame is just asleep,
And steel is strong because it knew the hammer and white heat.
These things shall pass and life be sweeter,
When faith and hope are strong they cannot long endure.

People may be experiencing rough times. But knowing "these things shall pass," provides hope for the future that can bring encouragement for the present. This is the underlying thought in a country music classic you may have heard in years past. It tells the story of a poor cotton picker, living in poverty, barely able to get by. Food is scarce, his kids need shoes, his wagon needs repair. But he *looks forward* to "pick'n time," when things will be better.

A couple verses given here will express the overall feeling expressed in the song:

It's hard to see by the coal oil light,
And I turn it off pretty early at night,
Cause a jug of coal oil costs a dime,
But I'll stay up late comes pick'n time!

Last Sunday morning when they passed the hat,
It was still nearly empty back where I sat,
But the preacher smiled and said, "That's fine,
The Lord will wait till pick'n time!"

People who always have something to look forward to—for the joy set before them—are able to cope. Those who have nothing to look forward to, can easily become discouraged.

13

A tremendous example of what looking forward can do for a person, is well illustrated in the life of Jacob who agreed to labor seven years for the girl he loved. "And Jacob served seven years for Rachel; *and they seemed unto him but a few days,* for the love he had to her" (Gen. 29:20). For the joy that was set before him, he sailed through the work he faced. His looking forward, his anticipation, kept him from bogging down in discouragement and defeat.

Let me give you a similar, but simple, modern-day example. A father told his teen-age son that he had to mow the lawn that afternoon when he got home from school. The boy didn't like mowing the lawn. He made all kinds of excuses in his mind—he was too tired, too busy, etc. Then his girlfriend came by and asked if he could go play tennis! Knowing he had to mow the lawn before he would be

allowed to play tennis, he suddenly got with it!

Because of "the joy that was set before him" he now had *incentive*. To be able to do the thing he wanted to do, helped him through the job he didn't want to do.

How might this principle work for us?

A person could tell himself: I have this unpleasant job to do, but I am going to get in and get it done. Instead of taking all day to do it, I will be done early. Then I will be good to myself: I will take this extra time to do something I *like* to do! This sets up an incentive factor. By this method one can use the pleasant thing for leverage to accomplish the unpleasant thing.

As in the case of the young man mowing the lawn first, the wise policy is to take care of the unpleasant task *first,* and save the pleasant thing for later—*so there is always something to look forward to.*

A person planning a trip may "go now and pay later." But normally it would be better to do the unpleasant part—save up the money first—and then go and enjoy it. This way, while saving up for the trip, one can look forward to it.

In hiking, if the trail heads *up* the mountain going, then the return is easier, being downhill. I personally prefer this over a trail down into a steep canyon, for then it is *up hill all the way back!* Better to do the strenuous part when fresh; the easier part when tired.

When some people eat watermelon, they purposely save the heart until last.

A child may be encouraged to eat his supper, knowing that a reward will be a

special dessert he likes! But he must eat his supper *first!* He may not like his vegetables, but "for the joy set before him" —the ice cream—he obtains the necessary incentive.

In life, in many ways, anticipation provides incentive. It is the story of a man who works hard digging a well, looking forward to striking water—or a prospector who continues to dig, looking forward to finding gold—or a college student who digs ditches now, so he will not have to dig ditches later!

People always function better when they have something to *look forward to*. Throughout the day, some may be looking forward to a television program they plan to watch that night. They may be looking forward to something they have ordered through the mail. They may be looking forward to read-

ing a new book or magazine. They may be looking forward to some special meetings planned for their church. They may be looking forward to a visit with a friend or a phone call from a special person.

In my own life, at any given time, I am looking forward to things—various speaking engagements, travel, attending a conference, meeting people, visiting friends and relatives, a research project, writing a new book, etc.

Some couples keep romance in their marriage because they are always looking ahead, planning special times

together. Such times need not be elaborate or expensive to be special. It might be a picnic in the woods or by a lake. It might be a dinner at home with their favorite food. The wife may set the table especially nice and light a couple candles. Throughout the day, both look forward to this little celebration they have planned. But what are they celebrating? It need not be some monumental thing—they may just celebrate because they read this suggestion! Why not?

We live in a complex and busy society. Some find relief from this by engaging in simple things such as planting seeds and looking forward to seeing a garden spring to life.

A rut has been defined as "a grave with both ends knocked out of it." This is where a lot of people are. Suppose a trip is planned to go visit relatives. Instead of taking the same route that may have been travelled many times, why not go a different way?

To give a personal example that comes to mind, having on many occasions travelled the highway over the mountains from Los Angeles to Bakersfield, which is now designated as Interstate 5, we decided to take the old route, known in years past as the Grapevine Grade or Ridge Route. Driving along this road on the poured concrete sections with its narrow width and sharp curves, one could imagine the Model T Fords of a bygone era as they maneuvered the grade! Though there was no traffic on the old road, it was definitely slower. But it was different!

Some years ago a man wrote a series of books on the back roads of California. His books were not about Disneyland, Yosemite National Park, or San Francisco, all of which are already well-known. Instead, he zeroed in on many little-known places which were interesting because of their uniqueness or historical significance. With a little research or inquiry, such places can be visited and are often not that far out of the way!

17

An example of this—and again we are back on Interstate 5 going north from Los Angeles—would be Fort Tejon. Millions of people travel this route each year. As they zoom by at 55 miles per hour (or faster!), the vast majority do not realize that only a few hundred feet from the freeway, near the summit, are the buildings of the historical fort. Here, to guard the pass, the government stationed soldiers whose transportation was provided by camels! This was long before highways and automobiles. On some weekends, incidents of those earlier days are re-enacted, complete with the firing of cannons and people dressed in costumes of that period.

The mountains on this route are not especially attractive. Though they can get snow at one season, and be green at another, much of the year they are brown and dull. But in the spring, sections of these mountains are ablaze with color, carpeted with poppies in abundance! A trip planned for this time, either as a destination in itself, or with this in mind, could provide a "looking forward" dimension.

Now what I am saying is this. A visit to some interesting place along the way can turn what might otherwise be a dull trip, especially for children, into something to look forward to. Such a trip might include a picnic by a stream, a hike to a waterfall, a few minutes to throw a frisbee or ball—perhaps to fly a kite from some breezy knoll!

What is true in natural things, is also true in spiritual things for the family of God. We must not get into a religious rut. "Every end is a new beginning," are the words on a little plaque hanging in our home. Instead of mourning about "what could have been *if only*..." we need to allow God to do a "new thing" in us (cf. Isa. 43:19). We need to let go of thoughts and things which are no longer productive and which erode the positive flow of God's blessings. Past hurts, losses, disappointments, and trials must be left behind as we pass through new doors and develop new relationships. Instead of looking back in regret, we must look forward with anticipation!

A church that has a vision—is winning souls, is growing, is building, is looking forward—is a vibrant and victorious church. But a church that no longer has a vision, that is not moving along in the flow of the Holy Spirit, will soon dry up. "Where there is no vision, the people perish" (Pro. 29:18).

As Christians we are admonished to look forward, "forgetting those things which are behind, and reaching forth unto those things which are *before*." By so doing, we "press toward the mark for the prize of the high calling of God" (Phil. 3:13, 14). "Let us *go on* unto perfection" (Heb. 6:1). Let us *"follow on* to know the Lord" (Hosea 6:3). Let us *"grow* in grace, and in the knowledge of our Lord" (2 Pet. 3:18). There is no standing still in God's program, it is a looking forward, a moving on up experience.

Some will remember C.M. Ward, for many years the speaker on the "Revivaltime" radio program. I once heard him say that if he were putting a hymn book together, he would include the theme song from "The Jeffersons," MOVING ON UP! In the television series "moving on up" was apparently a move to a high-rise building and success. As followers of Christ, we should be moving on up, spiritually speaking, with more of his truth, more of his love, more of his kindness, more of HIM!

A small child may look forward to the start of school. A young person may look forward to being able to

drive a car. There is a looking forward to graduation, marriage, children, a career—for young people.

But when people get older and feel their life is behind them, it becomes more difficult to look forward. They may become discouraged and despondent. What is the answer? The answer is to deliberately set up things in one's life, so there is always something to look forward to. Pursue a hobby, get involved in volunteer work, take a college course, find something to do, and do it!

I knew an elderly man once who told me he might have ended up sitting around doing nothing. But because his dog wanted to go for walks, he daily was out and about, a practice that contributed to his physical and mental well-being.

Or, let me tell you about Jack, a man I knew twenty-five years ago who lived in Fresno, California. Jack was a fine Christian man who often sent offerings to my ministry. He sold a piece of property across from his house to McDonald's for a fast-food restaurant. He was up in years and was not hurting for money (especially after this sale!). But when McDonald's was about to open, he went over and applied for a job! Soon he was making hamburgers, frying fries, and waiting on customers. He was by far the oldest employee, but he enjoyed working with the young people and they enjoyed him also. Time was not dragging for him now. Each day he looked forward to the challenge of the fast-food business.

Old age, even with its problems and challenges, should not be a time of depression, *certainly not for a Christian.* For while in one sense, much of one's life is behind, in another sense—an overwhelmingly greater sense—one's life is ahead: ETERNAL LIFE IN CHRIST!

"O death, where is thy sting? O grave, where is thy victory?.... Thanks be to God, who gives us the victory through our Lord Jesus Christ. Therefore, my beloved brethren, be stedfast, unmoveable, always abounding in the work of the Lord, forasmuch as you know that your labor is not in vain in the Lord" (1 Cor. 15:55-58).

"Now are we the sons of God, and it doth not yet appear what we shall be: but we know that, when he shall appear, we shall be like him; for we shall see him as he is" (1 John 3:2).

What a day that will be! There will be no more sickness or suffering; no more problems or pain; no more frustration or fear; no more destruction or death!

This is something to look forward to!

Chapter 3

POWER GREATER THAN THE PROBLEM

—by Ralph Woodrow

The Bible often tells of men and women who—like ourselves—had problems. Noah, Moses, Elijah, Peter and Paul all had problems. But, the Bible is also the account of how these people trusted in God, and his power proved to be greater than their problems.

Are you facing a problem right now? Perhaps it is a problem in your home or on the job; perhaps it is a physical or emotional problem. Perhaps you don't know which way to turn. The problem may be so sensitive that you hesitate to even share it with anyone else. Whatever the problem may be, I want to say that God's POWER is greater than your PROBLEM, greater than all the problems of this world put together!

Let me give you five "power" verses. God has promised us:

"...*power* to become the sons of God" (John 1:12).

"...*power* of God unto salvation" (Rom. 1:16).

"...*power* over all the power of the enemy" (Lk. 10:19).

"...*power* after that the Holy Ghost is come upon you" (Acts 1:8).

"...*power* that worketh in us"—abundant power (Eph. 3:20).

The last of these verses, a great preaching text, says that God "is able to do exceeding abundantly above all that we ask or think, according to the power that worketh in us."

In this great chapter (Ephesians 3), the apostle speaks in glowing terms of—

"the mystery of Christ...now-revealed,"

"the unsearchable riches of Christ,"

"the manifold wisdom of God,"

"the eternal purpose,"

"the love which passeth knowledge,"

"being filled with all the fullness of God"!

Then—as if these things were not enough!—he comes to this verse, Ephesians 3:20, speaking of God's unlimited power, power exceeding and abundant above all we can ask or think, and declares that this power is working in us!

This power "worketh." It is a living, vital, present-tense operation of the Spirit. It works! Notice, also, this divine power is not far off in heaven. It works "in us." God has chosen to place this treasure in earthen vessels. He has poured out of his Spirit into his people. This is why the Bible says, "Greater is he that is in you" (1 John 4:4). "If God be for us, who can be against us?...In all these things we are MORE THAN CONQUERORS through Him" (Rom. 8:31,37).

The word translated "power" in Ephesians 3:20 is "dunamis," the same Greek word from which the word "dynamite" comes! Surely, there is something explosive about this power!

If we were to make a list of our problems, how many would be on the list? Let me tell you about a man in the Bible, Shamgar by name, who was confronted with 600 problems! That is probably more than we would have on our list!

Shamgar is not as famous as Moses, Elijah, or Paul. Sermons are seldom preached about him. No movies have been made about him. We don't hear of "The Last Temptation of Shamgar" or about his "Robe"! While we do not know much about Shamgar, we do know this: when he was confronted with an overwhelming set of problems, he considered not the problem, but the power!

Facing 600 Philistines he could have easily given up in defeat. Imagine a battle with six hundred men against one! What should he do? If he ran, sooner or later, one of them would have caught him. Certainly such a challenge required more than *self*-confidence! Faith in GOD was the need of the hour.

Shamgar had very little with which to fight. All he had in his hand was an insignificant ox goad. It was no divine relic. It had never performed any miracles. It had only driven oxen along a dusty road. But Shamgar *took what he had.* This is the secret. He took what he had and began to use it in faith, with the result that all his enemies were defeated (Jud. 3:31).

What is that in *your* hand? I firmly believe the answer is not far off or impossible to reach (cf. Rom. 10:8). There is something in your hand or within reach—right *now*— that can deal a blow for deliverance. Take what is in *your* hand and begin to use it for God. Use the step you are *now* on to go higher.

Then there is the case of Samson who had one thousand problems! "And he found a new jawbone of an ass, and took it, and slew a thousand men therewith" (Jud. 15:15). We should not suppose Samson did these things because he was a giant or had some superior physical advantage. When the Spirit of God departed from him, he was like any other man (Jud. 16:19,20).

When he faced a thousand enemies, all that he had with which to work was a worthless jawbone. It had never accomplished any miracles. But this is what he had and he used what he had in faith. He didn't consider the problem; he considered the power.

Have you ever felt you were outnumbered? Have you felt the problem was too great? Perhaps you have tried to run from the problem. But, like Shamgar and Samson, there is something within your reach—whoever you are—which can be used to solve the problem, to turn tragedy into triumph. Take what you have and use it for God.

Though we may feel insignificant, remember "our sufficiency is of God" and "God is able to make all grace abound toward you; that you, always having all sufficiency in all things, may abound unto every good work" (2 Cor. 3:5; 9:8). What a promise!

Some problems are so complex and complicated—one gets the feeling that whichever way things go, defeat cannot be avoided. Such was the situation described in Amos 5:19: "A man did flee from a lion, and a bear met him;

he went into the house, and leaned his hand on the wall, and a serpent bit him." Sometimes it seems that no matter which way we turn or what we do, we can't win for losing! But with God on our side, *we cannot lose for winning!* He has the answer to the problem no matter how complicated it may seem. There is a way out!

Some problems become especially complicated because they involve *other* people. Take the case of a young woman who had become a Christian. Her husband hated God, the church, and anything connected with the church. He told her that if she went to church one more time, he would kill her. Having a mean disposition and insane temper, such words provided a definite threat. She knew the biblical admonition that we are not to forsake assembling ourselves together. She felt her need, and the need of her children, for the church and spiritual worship there. On the other hand, she did not want to be killed! Her children and their welfare were of great concern to her. What should she do?

A pastor I know was offered a large church in southern California, one of the largest in his denomination at the time. When he met with the church board, a certain problem was explained to him. A man and woman—each holding positions in the church—were romantically involved. Both were married, but not to each other. Neither the other husband  nor wife knew about this. The board members explained their concerns to the prospective pastor, pointing out that exposure of this situation could easily erupt into a church split. The parties involved had children, teenagers, who could also be seriously hurt.

What should a pastor do in a case like this? Is it not true that "a little leaven leavens the whole lump"? (1 Cor. 5:6). Should he "cry aloud and spare not" as Isaiah was told to do on one occasion? (Isa. 58:1). Or, could it be that allowing "space to repent" (Rev. 2:21) could provide time for things to turn around without taking drastic measures? Should he allow the wrong to continue, at least for a while, for the sake of the overall body of people, the children, and others that would be hurt were the matter exposed and dealt with immediately?

Answers to such problems, humanly speaking, are not easy. But when a person faces a problem so complex that whichever way he turns no solution seems possible—when there is a bear in one direction, a lion in another, and over here is a snake (Amos 5:19)—there is still one way to turn. Turn to God! He specializes in things thought impossible, he can do what no other power can do.

One time the prophet Elisha was faced with a problem like this. It seemed there was no way to turn, no way out. He was completely surrounded by an enemy army! There was a reason for this. Every time the Syrians would make a move against Israel, God would reveal it to the prophet and their advance would end in defeat. Consequently those Syrian soldiers were getting nervous in the service and having hysterics in the barracks!

The king suspected that one of his men was giving out military secrets, that someone—to use a modern day expression —"had let the cat out of the bag." But then someone told him what was going on. There was a prophet in Israel that knew every move he would make—that even the words he spoke in the "bedcham-  ber" were no secret to Elisha! Consequently, the Syrian king knew that until he got the prophet out of the way, he would gain no victory against Israel!

So he sent an entire *army* with horses and chariots to get one preacher! During the night they surrounded the town of Dothan where Elisha was staying. The next morning, Elisha's assistant rose and saw the problem they faced. "Alas, my master!" he cried, "how shall we do?" He almost had an instantaneous nervous breakdown! He was considering the problem, not the power!

But Elisha considered the power. "Fear not," he answered, "for *they that be with us are more than they that be with them"!* (2 Kings 6:16). Another great preaching text!

27

When the spiritual eyes of Elisha's helper were opened, he too could see that the mountain was filled with horses and chariots of fire—armies from outer space!—symbols of God's protective power from heaven. Finally, what seemed like such an impossible problem was solved by divine power, resulting in a great victory!

Now what about us? How many problems are we facing? If we made a list, just how many problems would there be? Shamgar had six hundred problems. Samson had one thousand. We don't have that many!

The question is asked in Genesis 18:14: "Is anything too hard for the Lord?" Centuries later, Jeremiah answered that question. "Ah Lord God! behold! thou hast made the heaven and the earth by thy great power...*there is nothing too hard for thee*" (Jer. 32:17).

"With GOD all things are possible" (Matt. 19:26) and "if you have faith...nothing shall be impossible unto YOU"! (Matt. 17:20)—for God "is able to do exceeding abundantly above all that we ask or think, according to the POWER that worketh in US"! (Eph. 3:20).

What a contrast there is between the man who dwells on the problem and the man who believes God's power is greater than the problem. The "problem" man is discouraged and defeated; the "power" man rejoices and is victorious, knowing that God's power can turn tragedy to triumph!

Chapter 4

TRIUMPHANT PRAYER

—by Arlene Woodrow

One day my mother-in-law, Florence Woodrow, and I were sharing regarding what parts of the newspaper we read. She named three or four sections she rarely misses, one of them being the obituaries—now that sounds rather morbid! But, she went on to explain, having lived in Riverside most of her life, she has been acquainted with many local people over the years—school friends, teachers, neighbors, church members, store clerks, and others. Consequently obituaries were not without significance.

This conversation reminded me of a death notice I saw recently—one that brought back feelings of nostalgia and sorrow. Perhaps you also knew the deceased. Because friends of the deceased may be interested, we reprint the death notice:

OBITUARY: MRS. PRAYER MEETING IS DEAD

Mrs. Prayer Meeting died recently at the First Neglected Church, on Worldly Avenue. Born many years ago in the midst of great revival, she was a strong healthy child, fed largely on testimony and Bible study, soon growing into worldwide prominence. She was one of the most influential members of the famous Church family. For the past several years Sister Prayer Meeting had been failing in health, gradually wasting away until rendered helpless by stiffness of knees, coldness of heart, inactivity, and weakness of purpose.

29

At the last she was but a shadow of her former happy self. Her last whispered words were inquiries concerning the strange absence of her loved ones now busy in the marts of trade and places of worldly amusements.

Experts, including Dr. Works, Dr. Reform, and Dr. Joiner, disagreed as to the cause of her fatal illness, administering large doses of organization, socials, contests and drives, but to no avail. A postmortem showed that a deficiency of spiritual food, coupled with a lack of faith, heart-felt religion, and general support, were contributing causes. Only a few were present at her death, sobbing over memories of her past beauty and power. (Source Unknown)

Not only is this a "clever" way to say something—but unfortunately, it is more truth than fiction. Certainly, there *are* churches and individuals that continue effective prayer ministries. However, at the same time, it seems comparatively few are involved in the kind of travailing prayer and spiritual warfare that brings lasting deliverance and revival. Too often people espouse Christianity without the life-changing phenomenon that makes a dramatic difference between the world and the church. It has been said, "The world has become so churchy, and the church has become so worldly, you can't tell the difference."

There is a time when church business must be transacted. But if members of a church board know more about *by-laws* than the *Bible,* if *politics* become more important than spiritual *power,* and if the *business* meeting replaces the *prayer* meeting, the church is in trouble!

Every great move of God has been spawned in an atmosphere in which prayer was a priority. As people have sought the Lord, they have received His joy, His righteousness, His love. His vision for the needs of a lost

30

and dying world has transformed them into vibrant prayer warriors who intercede for the salvation and deliverance of others. Revival—not brought in an evangelist's briefcase, but poured out by God—has been the result!

I'm so glad that the resurrecting power of Jesus Christ is able to raise up "Mrs. Prayer Meeting" from the dead!

Throughout the Gospels we see Jesus praying. He anguished in prayer alone. He prayed with and for others. His ministry was saturated in prayer. If even *Jesus* needed to pray for strength, power, and wisdom for effective ministry, certainly *we* need to pray!

His disciples observed His effective prayer life—day after day communing with the Father and interceding for others. They sensed that His prayer life set Him on a higher plane. They knew their prayer lives were inadequate and ineffective in comparison—they hungered for the spiritual power that emanated from Him. Their response: *"Teach us to pray"* (Lk. 11:1). May that be our hearts' cry.

Jesus did teach them to pray—and He prayed *for* them. "Satan has desired to have you, that he may sift you as wheat," he said, "but I have prayed for you, that your faith fail not" (Lk. 22:31,32). Later, Jesus not only prayed for the disciples, but for *us* who would believe as a result of their ministries: "Neither pray I for these alone, but for them *also* which shall believe on me through their word" (Jn. 17:20). Even today, he *continues* to intercede on our behalf: "Wherefore He is able also to save them to the uttermost that come unto God by Him, seeing He ever liveth *to make intercession for them"* (Heb. 7:25; Rom. 8:34).

There are some who would consider it very powerful to know that some great man of God or glorified saint was praying for them. But we are assured of more than this: *Jesus himself makes intercession for us!* It is a powerful truth.

The Bible says: "The Spirit also helpeth our infirmities: for we know not what we should pray for as we ought: but *the Spirit himself maketh intercession for us* ...according to the will of God" (Rom. 8:26-27). With that kind of intercession behind us, how can we help but succeed in *our* prayer life?!

Prayer is invading the impossible! This is not only the title of a book by Jack Hayford—it is a *fact.* All in whom the Spirit of God resides (all Christians) are called to intercessory prayer! It is not some mystical way-out wailing for a few "super-spirituals." It is simply standing in the gap between darkness and light, between bondage and freedom, between death and life, between the kingdom of Satan and the Kingdom of God. This kind of prayer turns TRAGEDY INTO TRIUMPH!

Many years ago, after a challenging sermon on Christian service, my grandmother went to her pastor and apologetically explained that she felt inadequate to teach or take some major position. "The only thing I can do is pray," she told him. Knowing of her faithful part in the prayer ministry of the Church, the pastor was shocked that she felt her ministry was of lesser value. "Why Mrs. Ely," he responded, "you are doing the most important work in this Church! God would not be doing the mighty things that we see here, if it were not for people like you who are faithful in intercessory prayer!"

Paul taught that the Christian should have on the complete "armor of God"—with truth buckled about the waist, the breastplate of righteousness, feet shod with the gospel, the shield of faith, the helmet of salvation, and the sword of the Spirit—yet even with all this protection, *showing the importance of prayer,* he goes on to say: "...praying always with all prayer and supplication in the Spirit, and watching thereunto with all perseverance and supplication for all saints" (Eph. 6:11-18).

As soldiers in the Lord's army, through prayer we are able to ward off the attacks of the enemy—to "put him on the run"! The power of prayer puts the pray-er on the offensive—making the attack—while the devil is on the defensive. Like a "bully," he takes off when he sees he isn't dealing with scared "sissies"! As James phrased it: "Submit yourselves to God. Resist the devil and *he will flee from you*" (Jam. 4:7).

Prayer *changes* things! I've heard it said, "Prayer doesn't change things, it changes the pray-er." Well, it does change the pray-er, but I have seen prayer change things, too! "The effectual fervent prayer of a righteous man availeth much" (James 5:16). Our prayers do make a difference. Why else would Paul have instructed Timothy with these words?

> "I exhort therefore, that, first of all, supplications, prayers, intercessions, and giving of thanks, be made for all men; for kings, and for all that are in authority; that we may lead a quiet and peaceable life in all godliness and honesty. For this is good and acceptable in the sight of God our Savior" (I Tim. 2:1-4).

Our praying can make the difference in quality of life for ourselves, our families, and all within reach of our prayers. Paul stated that prayer would make it possible to lead quiet and peaceable lives of godliness and honesty. Certainly our world needs more of that kind of prayer!

If more Christians would "sigh and cry for all the abominations that are done" in the land (Eze. 9:4), I believe the tide of drugs, crime, abortions, gang killings, serial murders, kidnappings, child pornography, and all kinds of filth could be turned around. Clearly prayer is an essential part of God's formula for the healing of a land (2 Chron. 7:14). It is good to get involved, and it is good to let our voice be heard, but the bottom line is that more can be accomplished through prayer than by waving banners and marching in protest. It is impossible to force Christian standards upon the unregenerate.

I have heard it said that we should "Pray like it all depends on God, and work like it all depends on us."

True—we should not always sit back and "do nothing" if our involvement can make a difference, but the most effective half of that couplet is PRAYER!

"But," you say, "I have prayed—and it didn't work!" Prayer isn't like "writing to Santa Claus" or "getting three wishes"! To hear some people talk, one would think God is most concerned with answering prayers (or wishes, if you please) for fancy cars, expensive houses, designer clothes, and ocean cruises. James mentioned that kind of prayer:

> "You ask, and receive not, because you ask amiss, that ye may consume it upon your lusts....Do you not know that the friendship of the world is enmity with God? Whosoever therefore will be a friend of the world is the enemy of God....Submit yourselves therefore to God" (Ja. 4:3-8).

God does provide our needs and even many of the "wants" if we "seek first the Kingdom of God." However, it is obvious throughout the Scriptures that our desires and prayers should be for eternal things rather than those things that "moth and rust corrupt...where thieves break through and steal...for where your treasure is, there will your heart be also" (Mt. 6:19-20).

Paul set a good example. He learned to be content in whatever state he found himself, whether he had little or much, knowing that he could live under any conditions through Christ who gave him strength (Ph. 4:11-13). Not too surprisingly, I have observed over the years that it isn't unusual for some people to be more victorious with little (when they have to depend on God for sustenance) than with much. Too often involvement with "things" erodes more important activities.

But, what about unanswered prayers for wayward loved ones, family trauma, healing, and other serious problems? Often we do see speedy answers to these serious needs, but we will have to admit that sometimes we pray faithfully for days, weeks, months and maybe

34

even years before "prayer changes things." A few reasons why prayers seem to go unanswered are discussed below:

• God does not force people to do something against their wills. When we anguish in prayer over others who obstinately go their own way, the answer may come slower or in a different way.

• Some of our trials actually cause us to grow in character—without those experiences we would never mature spiritually. God is not obligated to spoil His children by giving them everything that avoids discomfort in the process of "stretching."

• Unseen spiritual forces are sometimes interfering, as in the case of Daniel who had to wait twenty-one days while Michael overcame the evil power (Dan. 10:10-21).

• Some situations are very complex. God may be performing some long-term miracle that can only be recognized in retrospect. That kind of answer is usually remembered and appreciated far more than the instant miracles we all like to receive. Too often, what comes easy is also easily forgotten!

There are times when we may feel discouraged while we are waiting for an answer.

"But they that wait upon the Lord shall renew their strength; they shall mount up with wings as eagles; they shall run, and not be weary; and they shall walk, and not faint" (Isa. 40:31).

God is always there to encourage us, and bring us through to victory if we will only listen to His still small voice whispering deep within!

"Thou art my servant, I have chosen thee, and not cast thee away. Fear thou not; for I am with thee: be not dismayed; for I am thy God: I will strengthen thee; yea, I will help thee; yea, I will uphold thee with the right hand of my righteousness...and they that strive with thee shall perish...they that war against thee shall be as nothing, and as a thing of nought. For I the Lord thy God will hold thy right hand, saying unto thee, Fear not; I will help thee" (Isa. 41:9-13).

I have discovered that God does care—He does hear our prayers and He does answer! The answer may be

35

"yes," "no," or "wait." He may remove our "mountains," or help us to climb over, tunnel through, or go around the obstacles that hinder us. He always knows what is best! During the long process of "waiting" something good is happening inside the pray-er: We become *acquainted* with God as we spend time with Him. We learn a new dimension of *fellowship* with Him. We learn to sit at His feet and worship Him.

Instead of always thinking in terms of what we can get from God, we might consider a paraphrase of a famous quote, "Ask not what God can do for you, but what you can do for your God"—we can give him our love, praise, worship, and adoration. In the end, the pray-er gains tremendous strength and is then ready for God to answer his or her heart's cry!

Prayer of Adoration

O God, to sit before Thee,
  and breathe Thy Breath
Dost thrill and quicken me,
  and to "self" bring death!

Not with petitions sad and long,
  do I come to Thy Throne,
But with praise and a song,
  doth my soul in ecstasy groan!

Fulfillment, sweet fulfillment,
  enraptures this soul of mine,
Enveloped in You with deep sentiment—
  as my body of clay with Thee dost dine!

—Arlene Woodrow

Some years ago, when I was crying out to God to help me through overwhelming spiritual hurdles, God breathed into me words of encouragement that gave me strength to "hang on" when I felt I would surely fall. He can do the same for you! The secret is to spend time fellowshipping and communing with Him. You can converse with Him any place and any time, not only when you kneel to pray—but as you go about your day's activities, include Him. *He's always there.* Tell Him all about your

36

dilemma—then be still and LISTEN! Whether He guides you to the written Word or simply speaks to your heart as you bask in His presence, you will know when you have heard from Him. Your "situation" may not change immediately—but the hope you sense, and your new ability to cope, will carry you through until your faith and His faithfulness bring complete victory.

I conclude by sharing some of the words He spoke to me. I can tell you—it is true. He has been faithful—and has never let me down.

Be Still My Child

Trials and temptations come my way;
I falter and fail—
    and of my goals I nearly lose sight.
Darkness and pain and turmoil I feel!
THEN HE WHISPERS:
Be still my child—for I am God!
For thy good these trials have come,
To purify you like gold—this fire has come!
Don't despair—turn not thy back;
Lean not to thine own understanding,
But in all thy ways acknowledge thy God,
And I will direct thy paths!
This, too, shall pass and stronger you'll be!
Remember, my child—
In your weakness my strength is made known!
Lean on me and draw from my strength!
Read my Word! Fast and pray!—
And your soul's enemy will turn and run!
Wait before me and be still my child
    —for I am God!
       BE STILL MY CHILD!

—Arlene Woodrow

Chapter 5

"7-UP"

—by Ralph Woodrow

In 1929 it was called Bib-label Lithiated Lemon Lime Soda. Today, we know this soft drink as 7-UP. But this message is not about a carbonated beverage; it is about seven "ups" of the Bible. Our title may not sound too deep, theologically speaking, nevertheless messages with simple titles may be long remembered when others fade into obscurity. I have actually had the experience of meeting people I had not seen in years who would say: "We remember when you came to our church years ago as a young preacher—you spoke on Seven Up!"

There are seven points to this message which I will state at the outset: (1) Wake up, (2) Shake up, (3) Pay up, (4) Make up, (5) Fire up, (6) Cheer up, and (7) Shut up.

1. WAKE UP. "Now it is high time to *awake* out of sleep: for now is our salvation nearer than when we believed. The night is far spent, the day is at hand: let us therefore cast off the works of darkness" (Rom. 13:11, 12). Paul says it is time to *wake up.*

It is through the church that God is able to do "exceedingly abundantly above all we can ask or think" (Eph. 3:20). Yet, the church has sometimes been asleep—as a sleeping giant. The potential is there. The power is there. The authority is there. But a sleeping church will not get the job done.

In Ephesians 5:14, we read: "Wherefore he saith, '*Awake* thou that sleepest, and arise from the dead, and Christ shall give thee light'." Normally we would assume this is a quotation from the Old Testament. But it is not found anywhere in the Old Testament. It has been conjectured it may have been a part of a Christian hymn that was then in use. In any event, the message is that people must wake up.

The prophet Joel said: "Blow the trumpet in Zion, and sound an *alarm* in my holy mountain" (Joel 2:1). What is the purpose for an alarm? It is to wake people up. An *alarm* clock is a clock that wakes people up. Preachers who fail to sound

the alarm, to give the warning, to wake us up, do not measure up to God's standards. Isaiah had a name for them: "They are dumb dogs, they cannot bark; sleeping, lying down, loving to slumber" (Isa. 56:10). Imagine having a watch dog that sleeps all the time—a dog that does not bark when some intruder comes near!

Jesus told a parable about "a man which sowed good seed in his field: but *while men slept,* his enemy came and sowed tares among the wheat, and went his way" (Matt. 13:24,25). Had these men been awake, they could have stopped this trespassing and prevented the disaster that resulted later on. So is it with us. While we sleep, spiritually speaking, the enemy plants his seeds. We do not realize what has happened at the time, but later these seeds become weeds!—weeds of compromise, bitterness, malice, envy, variance, jealousy, and strife. They grow and begin to choke out the good in our lives.

Jesus said to his sleeping disciples, "Watch and pray, that you enter not into temptation: the spirit indeed is willing, but the flesh is weak" (Matt. 26:41). Needless to say, the flesh *is* weak. As the disciples on that occasion, we all need the spiritual reinforcement that is ours through prayer. When the church has gotten so worldly, and the world has gotten so churchy, we must wake up and take a look at our spiritual condition.

For some, spiritual things are no more important than a fad—like a diet for reducing or collecting antiques. They have "a form of godliness, but deny the power thereof" (2 Tim. 3:5). It is more than a little hot chocolate in the church basement. Sermonettes for Christianettes are not the answer. We should remember that "not every one that says Lord, Lord, shall enter into the kingdom of heaven, but he who does the  will of the Father which is in heaven" (Matt. 7:21). "In Christ...old things pass away; behold, all things become *new*" (2 Cor. 5:17). We need to wake up!

Isaiah preached: "Awake, awake...shake thyself from the dust" (Isa. 52:1,2). It was not "shake and bake," but "awake and shake"—which brings us to our next point.

2. SHAKE UP. Ezekiel once saw the house of Israel as a valley "full of bones, and lo, they were very dry." His description could well fit the spiritual condition of many churches. They need more than a "revival," it will take a *resurrection* for them, they are so dead! As Ezekiel told those dry bones to "hear the word of the Lord," there was "a noise and behold a *shaking,* and the bones came together, bone to his bone...and the breath came into them, and they lived, and stood up upon their feet, an exceeding great army" (Ezek. 37:1-10).

You may remember the words of an old negro spiritual about "dem bones, dem bones, dem dry bones, now hear the word of the Lord!" As the pitch of the song rises, it tells how the foot bone's connected to the shin bone, the shin bone's connected to the knee bone, the knee bone's connected to the leg bone, the leg bone's connected to the hip bone, etc., and they all hear the word of the Lord!

What a shaking there was in that valley of dry bones! The breath came into them. They became a great army. So today, the church must have a shaking, a mighty infilling of the Holy Spirit, to become a great army for God. Such was the "shake up" experienced by the church in the book of Acts. On one occasion, not only were they shaken, but "the place was shaken where they were assembled together; and they were all filled with the Holy Ghost, and spoke the word of God with boldness" (Acts 4:31).

I used to have a song leader who would read the instructions on a bottle of salad dressing in a restaurant:

"Shake well before using." Then, before using the salad dressing, *he* would proceed to shake. Of course it got a lot of laughs—and a few funny looks! Shaking the body will not make one more spiritual, but many Christians today need a good old-fashioned shaking by the power of God—to shake off lethargy, deadness, worldliness, unbelief, a critical spirit, and any other debris that robs of spiritual victory.

3. PAY UP. It should be recognized by all that we cannot buy the blessings of God. We are "not redeemed with corruptible things as silver and gold...but with the precious blood of Christ" (1 Pet. 1:18). When the Samaria sorcerer offered Peter money, supposing he could buy a

41

gift of God, Peter said: "To hell with you and your money! How dare you think you could buy the gift of God?" (Acts 8:20). These words are from the Phillips version which adds a footnote: "These are exactly what the Greek means. It is a pity that their real meaning is obscured by modern slang."

J.B. Phillips only translated the New Testament. Had he put out a version of the entire Bible, it could have been called "Phillips 66"!

One can read Peter's words in *any* translation—all make it clear that Peter had no time or patience with the idea that money could buy the gift of God.

Some people have been taught that what they plant is what they will get. If they plant potatoes, they will get potatoes—true enough. So if they plant dollars, by giving big offerings to certain ministries, God will give them dollars, lots of dollars!—something like playing a glorified slot machine. While it is true that God does bless people financially—and we would not exalt poverty as a goal—yet true giving is not giving to *get*. There have been abuses.

Nevertheless, the Bible does teach giving. God has already done so much for us and, in a definite sense, we need to *pay up!* As in Malachi's day, we might well ask the question: "Will a man rob God?" (Mal. 3:8). It is not that God needs the money. How could he? He owns everything. But there is a principle here, an attitude that is involved.

Jesus said: "It is more blessed to give than to receive" (Acts 20:35). Interestingly, this quotation is nowhere in the gospels, as we might suppose. We only know these

42

words of Jesus because Paul quoted them while speaking to the Ephesian elders.

Some people have never learned how to give to God. When the offering plate comes by, they pull out a little coin, squeeze it so tight that Abe Lincoln would think the Civil War was still on! Grudgingly they look at their "offering" and sing:

> *When we part I cannot grin;*
> *God be with you till we meet again!*

But God loves a *cheerful* giver! (2 Cor. 9:6,7). "Where your treasure is, there will your heart be also" (Matt. 6:21). God wants us to be a generous people—not a stingy people. We need to pay up!

4. MAKE UP. You may have heard sermons against makeup—about how Jezebel painted her face. Others point out, however, that she also took a bath and combed her hair. And there is the story about a man who had an old dilapidated barn. One day he painted it bright red. It looked better. So, it is countered, sometimes a little paint helps an old barn!

But our subject here is not cosmetics. By "make up," we are talking about people making things right! We must not harbor an unforgiving spirit.

I recall years ago a woman who had been wronged by a preacher over some financial dealings. She told me: "I will *never* forgive him!" But who did this attitude hurt? The preacher had moved to another state and was no longer in contact with her. Her unforgiveness did not hurt him—he knew nothing about it one way or the other. This refusal to forgive hurt *her!*

How often should we forgive? Seven times? Jesus said to forgive *seventy times seven!* (Matt. 18:22). He taught us to pray: "Our Father which art in heaven...forgive us our debts, as *we* forgive our debtors." It would not be very

43

1   **2**

3   **4**

Located in the Oratory at the base of the tower of the well-known Jerusalem landmark, the International YMCA, the stone bas-reliefs shown here illustrate the principle of reconcilation. 1. "If thou bring thy gift to the altar," 2. "and there rememberest that thy brother hath aught against thee," 3. "leave there thy gift before the altar, and go thy way; first be reconciled to thy brother," 4. "and then come and offer thy gift" (Matt. 5:23,24).

consistent for us to ask God to forgive us, if we refuse to forgive others. Paul put it this way: "Be kind one to another, tenderhearted, *forgiving one another*, even as God for Christ's sake has forgiven you" (Eph. 4:32). The concept of forgiveness is at the very heart of the gospel. God wants us to *make up!*

A Christian lady once said to me: "You don't know all the lies they tell on me!" I told her: "Well, half the lies they tell on you are not true anyhow!" It took her back for a moment, but she was good natured and smiled.

As we have pointed out, Christians should "pay up," but even their offering is not acceptable to God *if they need to make up.* As our accompanying illustration shows, *"first* be reconciled to thy brother, and *then* come and offer thy gift" (Matt. 5:24). Wrongs must be made right.

5. FIRE UP. "I would you were cold or hot," Jesus said to the Christians at Laodicea. "So then because you are lukewarm, and neither cold nor hot, I will spew you out of my mouth" (Rev. 3:15,16). Like those at Laodicea, many today are lukewarm in their spiritual dedication. They need to *fire up!*

The question has been asked: "If you were arrested for being a Christian, would there be enough evidence to convict you?"

Jesus said, "You shall be witnesses unto me" (Acts 1:8). Many are lukewarm in their witness for Christ. Oh if someone backed them up against the wall they would not deny the Lord, but they never go out of their way to share the gospel with others.

I am reminded of a Christian young man who spent several months working in a remote logging area. Knowing he would be among many rough and ungodly men, the church back home continually held him up in prayer. When he returned, they asked him how he had survived this time, being a Christian. "Oh just fine," he replied, *"they never found out!"*

45

Some church members are lukewarm in honesty. They would not go out and rob a bank. But suppose they are given too much change as they go through the checkout counter at the market. They shove the money in their pocket and out the door they go! While professing to be "saints," they act like "ain'ts"! Dad gets so mad at mom that he picks up a chair and throws it at her. She and the children duck just in time for it to crash into the wall plaque that says: "God Bless Our Home." Then we wonder why there is not more blessing on many homes!

People always like to go see a fire. It has been said, "Get the church on fire and the city will turn out to watch us burn!" Some people are so afraid of wildfire, they have no fire at all. Generally speaking, there are usually enough "wet blankets" around to put it out.

A man described a church he attended once as "The First Church of the Frigidaire." It was so cold, the chandeliers were made of icicles, the pews were lined with frost, and as he looked around, sitting next to him was a polar bear! At offering time, the ushers skated up and down the aisles on ice skates collecting cold cash! Everything about that church was cold.

God makes his ministers "a flame of fire" (Heb. 1:7). Jeremiah was so aflame with the word of the Lord, it was like a fire shut up in his bones. Even when he became discouraged, and at one point thought he would quit preaching, he could not: "I said, I will not make mention of him, nor speak any more in his name. But his word was in mine heart as a burning *fire shut up in my bones,* and I was weary with forbearing, and I could not stay" (Jer. 20:9). The word was like a fire—he had to let it out. He couldn't quit preaching, even if he wanted to!

We need that fire, that enthusiasm, that power of the Holy Spirit. Too long the Devil has pushed us around; it is time to massage his vertebra with some red hot religion. One preacher said: "I'm gonna stomp that ole Devil till I can't stomp him anymore; I'm gonna punch him till I can't punch any more; I'm gonna bite him until I don't have any teeth, and then, bless God, I'll just *gum him to death!*" The Bible says: "Resist the devil, and he will flee from you" (Jam. 4:7).

A church member, who previously had attended services regularly, stopped going. After a few weeks, the minister came to visit him one chilly evening. Guessing the reason for his pastor's visit, the man welcomed him, led him to a big chair near the fireplace and waited. The minister made himself comfortable, but said absolutely nothing. After some minutes, he took the fire tongs, carefully picked up a brightly burning ember, and placed it to one side of the hearth, all alone. Then he sat back in his chair, still silent.

The host watched all of this in quiet fascination. As the one lone ember's flame diminished, there was a momentary glow and then its fire was no more. Not a word had been spoken since the initial greeting. Just before the minister was ready to  leave, he picked up the cold, dead ember and placed it back in the middle of the fire, and immediately it began to glow once more with the light and warmth of the burning coals around it. As the pastor reached the door to leave, his host said, "Thank you so much for your visit and especially for your fiery sermon. I shall be back in church next week!"

6. CHEER UP. In the midst of a severe storm, when the light of the sun or moon had not been seen in days, among 276 people on a ship at sea, Paul said: "Sirs, be of *good cheer:* for I believe God" (Acts 27:25). He had received a directive from the Lord. Though the ship would be lost, their lives would all be spared. One person can make a difference—someone who encourages people to *cheer up!*

People face all kinds of problems and adversity. Often we have no idea the heavy loads some carry. They may be near the breaking point. A kind word of cheer may help them make it; whereas negative, discouraging talk might push them further down—like the proverbial straw that breaks the camel's back.

The early Christians were filled with the Holy Ghost and *joy* (Acts 13:52). They didn't go around with faces so long they could suck marbles out of a gopher hole. Long faces are OK on mules in Missouri, but no good on Christians in California! Cheering up is good for one's health, too. "A merry heart doeth good like a medicine, but a broken spirit drieth the bones" (Pro. 17:22).

God can give us that inward joy, even in the face of trials and tribulations. It was in this context of severe trial and testing that Peter said he could rejoice "with joy unspeakable and full of glory" (1 Peter 1:8). It was such inward joy that caused Paul and Silas, though shut up in a Philippian prison, to sing praises unto God at midnight (Acts 16:25). "God...giveth songs in the night" (Job 35:10). Jesus said: "In the world you shall have tribulation, but *be of good cheer,* I have overcome the world" (John 16:33).

7. SHUT UP. People who try to monopolize every conversation, who constantly interrupt others (as though they know more than anyone else), are very rude. They need to learn when to *shut up.* "A fool's voice is known by multitude of words" (Ecc. 5:3). "Let every man be swift to hear, slow to speak" (Jam. 1:19). Sometimes we all talk too much. We talk when we should listen.

Jesus said: "Every idle word that men shall speak, they shall give account thereof in the day of judgment. For by your words you shall be justified, and by your words you shall be condemned" (Matt. 12:36,37). I don't know that I fully understand this, but it is evident that God looks on sins of the tongue very seriously. James wrote: "The tongue is a fire, a world of iniquity...it defileth the whole body, and...is set on fire of hell"! (Jam. 3:6).

Sometimes even Christians will gossip about a host of people, and all the sins they are supposedly committing, and then end by saying: "I don't want you to think I am 'talking' about these people. I'm just telling you this so you will *know how to pray!*"

I recall an incident that happened years ago at a church where I was holding meetings. When prayer requests were taken, one lady said: "Folks, let's pray for Mr. Richards. That old reprobate really needs God. He's a drunk, a womanizer, and just no good." She did not know that Mr. Richards was sitting right behind her! He had not been inside the church in years. In the embarrassment, he got up and walked out. The pastor of the church leaned over to me and explained what had happened. It was unfortunate.

Back in the 50s it was often de-bated whether a preacher, or any other Christian, should have a television set. Churches that had stood against the movie theater, now felt the theater was coming into the living room. Instead of "television," some called it "hellevision." Anyhow, in this setting, a woman phoned a certain pastor and said: "Did you know that Pastor _____ got him a hell-e-vision?" The other pastor, even though he did not have a television himself, asked her:

"Is that so? Did someone tell you that on your hell-e-phone?" We will not attempt to judge this woman's motives—God is the judge of that. The point is: a television or a telephone is but a channel. It can be a channel for truth—or trash. If one sins by gossiping, it is sin whether it is done over the back fence to a neighbor or on a telephone to a person a thousand miles away.

If it is bad to gossip, it is also bad to listen to gossip. If someone says: "Did you hear what so-and-so did?" You can ask: "Was it good?" When their reply is negative, you can say: "Then I don't want to hear it!" Jesus said: "Take heed what you *hear*" (Mk. 4:24).

People who always put others down, must suppose that making others look small will make themselves look **BIG**. But there is no big **"I"** and little **"u"** in God's program. Each will give an account of himself to God. "Let your speech be always with grace, seasoned with salt, that you may know how you ought to answer every man" (Col. 4:6).

There is even a time when the preacher should shut up! It is inexcusable to say, "And now in closing..." and then continue the sermon another twenty minutes! I am reminded of the words of a little country preacher who prayed: "Lord, fill me with your stuff, and nudge me when I've said enough!"

It has been said: "There are *four* parts to a good sermon: (1) Tell them what you are going to tell them, (2) tell them, (3) tell them what you told them, and then (4) shut up." And having covered our seven points, we will do just that!

Chapter 6

TATTLERS AND BUSYBODIES

—by Arlene Woodrow

Have you heard? Now let me tell you—you wouldn't believe it! Now, I don't mean this as gossip—but I feel you should know.... "Remember Me?"—

My name is Gossip. I have no respect for Justice.
I maim without killing. I break hearts and ruin lives.
I am cunning and malicious and gather strength with age.
The more I am quoted the more I am believed.
I flourish at every level of society.
My victims are helpless.
They cannot protect themselves against me—
*   because I have no name and no face.*
To track me down is impossible.
The harder you try, the more elusive I become.
I am nobody's friend.
Once I tarnish a reputation, it is never quite the same.
I topple governments and wreck marriages.
I ruin careers, cause sleepless nights, heartache and
*   indigestion.*
I spawn suspicion and generate grief.
I make innocent people cry in their pillows.
Even my name hisses. I am called Gossip.
Office gossip. Shop gossip. Party gossip.
I make headlines and headaches.
Before you repeat a story ask yourself,
*   Is it true? Is it fair? Is it necessary?*
If not—SHUT UP.   —Author Unknown

Gossip is an ancient pastime. Evidently gossipers caused a lot of trouble as far back as the time of Moses, for he wrote: "Thou shalt not go up and down as a talebearer among thy people" (Lev. 19:16). Solomon wrote, "A talebearer revealeth secrets: but he that is of a faithful spirit concealeth the matter" (Prov. 11:13). "Pick your friends—but not to pieces!"

The principles illustrated by the three monkeys are so valid: see no evil, speak no evil, and hear no evil! (Mt. 6:23; 12:37; Mk. 4:24).

More people are run down by gossip than by cars! It happens not only over the back fence and behind closed doors—but also by phone, fax, radio and television (yes, even in the news)—and certainly through the sensational scandal publications that regurgitate filth at check-out counters.

Even some who would not normally take part in gossip seem to get some kind of titillation from reading about this or that politician, TV evangelist, movie star, or other victim of the latest garbage (which may be bold-faced lies). Some of it may be based on truth—but is often distorted beyond recognition. For that matter, what right do we have to indulge in the morsels of some poor soul's mistakes —even if it is true! Unfortunately, there must be a lucrative market for such human sludge—or these publishers would soon close up shop.

It has been said, "It is better to say a good thing about a bad fellow than to say a bad thing about a good fellow!"

Sometimes there are people who profess to be *Christians*—yet they gossip and tear others apart, or blow up when things don't go their way?! Hold it! Who are they trying to kid?—*their religion is vain!* "If any man among you seem to be religious, and bridleth not his tongue, but deceiveth his own heart, *this man's religion is vain.* Pure religion and undefiled before God and the

Father is this; to visit the fatherless and widows in their afflictions, and to keep himself unspotted from the world" (Jam. 1:26-27).

Instead of running people down, how much better to be a person who endeavors to lift others up! Why not reach out to someone less fortunate—someone who is having problems? How about giving a hand to the neighbors down the street?—the people whose kids are pests and their house ramshackle! Perhaps they live under difficult circumstances and there is a *reason* why they don't excel in living an orderly life. Your help and concern may be the little boost they need. It helps to know someone *cares!*

Gossip is often passed on by those who have nothing to do but sit around and talk about others. If one is busy doing and saying *good* and *right* things, there is little time to get into trouble. "And withal they learn to be idle, wandering about from house to house; and not only idle, but tattlers also and busybodies, speaking things which they ought not" (I Tim. 5:13).

There is plenty to do. If your days aren't full in putting food on your table and keeping your own home in order—consider getting busy with activities that will lighten someone's load and make you feel better, too. Try some of these:
Bake for a neighbor. Visit the sick or elderly—run some errands or help in the home. Visit or minister in a convalescent home. Take a bouquet to someone—or drop a note to one who may be having a "glad day" or a "bad day." Pick up your phone and just "check in" with a shut-in who rarely gets a call from someone who cares. Get involved in ministry—prayer, visitation, music, Christian education, youth work, secretarial duties, providing floral arrange-

ments to beautify the sanctuary, Bible studies for your work place or neighborhood. The list is *endless*!

People who busy themselves with activities that bless (instead of hurt) other people will find life much more rewarding! "Give and it shall be given unto you!" Give of yourself and people will give you their appreciation and love. If you choose to live this kind of life—you won't be prey to falling into the bad company that lurks in a run-down place called "Gossip Town."

> *Have you ever heard of Gossip Town,*
> *On the shores of Falsehood Bay,*
> *Where old Dame Rumor, with rustling gown,*
> *Is going the livelong day?*
> *It isn't far to Gossip Town*
> *For people who want to go;*
> *The Idleness train will take you down*
> *In just an hour or so.*
>
> *The "Thoughtless Road" is the popular route,*
> *And most people go that way;*
> *But it's steep down-grade; if you don't look out*
> *You will land in Falsehood Bay.*
> *You glide through the valley of Vicious Talk,*
> *And into the "Tunnel of Hate;"*
> *Then, crossing the "Add-To Bridge," you walk*
> *Right into the City Gate.*
>
> *The principal street is called "They Say,"*
> *And "I've Heard" is the public well,*
> *And the breezes that blow from Falsehood Bay*
> *Are laden with "don't you tell."*
> *In the midst of the town is "Tell Tale Park;"*
> *You are never quite safe while there,*
> *For its owner is Madam Suspicious Remark,*
> *Who lives on the street "Don't Care."*
>
> *Just back of the park is "Slanderer's Row;"*
> *'Twas there that Good Name died,*
> *Pierced by a shaft from Jealousy's bow,*
> *In the hands of Envious Pride.*
> *From Gossip Town, Peace long since fled,*
> *But Trouble and Grief and Woe*
> *And Sorrow and Care you'll meet instead,*
> *If you ever chance to go.*
>
> —Harvey M. Barr, *Out of My Treasure*, College Press, Joplin, MO.

You can't spell "brothers" and not spell "others."

If we're Christlike—we won't gossip and criticize others. We won't automatically think the worst or believe the dirt we hear. (If we knew the whole story, we may marvel that the object of attack could stand up under such circumstances.) Instead, let's go to our knees and pray for those whose lives are full of pain and hardship! That kind of prayer is most effective "in one's closet." It is self-righteous deception to pass along things that shouldn't be said, prefaced by: "I'm just telling you this because I want you to pray with me about this problem." Of course, it is good to "agree" in prayer, but, God is quite capable of answering our "confidential" prayers without muddying the water by involving a third party!

"The only people who have a right to be fault-finders—are people who study earthquakes!"

What makes us think we have less faults than the one we're slashing with our tongues? Are we hiding behind deadly nit-picking and criticism of others to cover up our own inadequacies and short-comings? The fires of hostility and fault-finding are often fanned more viciously toward those whose abilities and behavior actually surpass the gossipers. Paul said it well: "Brethren, if a man be overtaken in a fault, ye which are spiritual, restore such an one in the spirit of meekness; considering thyself, lest thou also be tempted" (Gal. 6:1).

> *There is so much bad in the best of us*
> *And so much good in the worst of us*
> *That it doesn't behoove any of us*
> *To talk about the rest of us!* —Author Unknown

It has been said, "Your tongue is in a wet place and is apt to slip!" If you don't want to do the things that cause trouble (for you as well as others), it is easier not to participate in slander and gossip, than to later try to unravel the mess once you open your mouth. I once heard it said, "You are master over your words until you speak them, then they are master over you." True!!

55

I know a pastor who had a lady in his church who had passed around malicious tales about him. The repercussions caused him extreme grief—and great damage was done to the church. In time, she began to feel convicted for her ungodly actions. She went to the pastor and grievously repented. He forgave her, prayed with her for God's forgiveness, and shared the following illustration:

A mischievous boy went up on the bell-tower of a church and ripped open a down-filled pillow. The tiny feathers were carried by the wind—slowly fluttering over many blocks. Later the boy felt sorry about the fuzzy little feathers that blanketed the town and decided it would be only right to clean up what he had spread.

Taking the empty pillow case in hand, he went up and down streets, through parks, behind buildings, reaching into nicks and crannies. Some were stuck to surfaces—up high, down low, out of reach—some had picked up dust and water along the way, resembling matted gunk more than dainty, fluffy down. Others would seem to take to the wind—just beyond reach. The repentant boy tried and tried to pick up all the feathers, but try as he may, he could not gather them all.

By the time the pastor completed his story, the woman was weeping. She realized, as never before, how impossible it is to retrieve rumors. It's best to "Button Up Your Lips"—

If you heard a bit of gossip, whether false or whether true,
Be it of a friend, or stranger, let me tell you what to do.
Button up your lips securely, lest the tale you should repeat,
And bring sorrow unto someone, whose life is not too sweet.
If you know of one who yielded to temptation long ago,
But whose life has since been blameless, let me tell you what to do.
Button up your lips securely, His the secret: God alone
Has the right to sit in judgment, treat it as to you unknown.
Sometimes life is filled with troubles, oft its burdens are severe,
Do not make it any harder by a careless word or sneer.
Button up your lips securely 'gainst the words that bring a tear,
Be swift with words of comfort, words of praise and words of cheer.
                                        —Author Unknown

I learned a big lesson in the 5th grade. I had never been in trouble nor sent to the office. I didn't lie, steal, hit others, or cause commotions in class. You can imagine my horror when I was called into the office. I had no idea what I had done, but had the feeling I was *in trouble.* (Why else was anyone called to the principal's office?!) In a cold sweat and trembling, I entered the office. The principal solemnly requested me to be seated. Sternly, she asked if I knew the meaning of a certain word. As I stammered, I felt *terrible*—and with  a rush of embarrassment and regret knew why I was there. I didn't fully comprehend what the word meant—but I had the idea that it was pretty bad.

It all started that morning when someone told me what "terrible" things a certain girl did. She was the sister of one of my classmates—much older and more experienced—a 6th grader! I can't remember why, but, during recess I repeated what I had heard. I didn't mean it maliciously. Yet, even at that tender age my conscience was pricked as I knew I said something about someone that I shouldn't have. To this day I have no idea if what I heard (and said) was *true* or not, but of this I'm sure—*I had no business repeating it!*

My classmate and her sister were pretty irate with me for a few days—and I became aware that "big mouths" or gossips could be despised. My early adverse experience with spreading rumors opened my eyes to how fast they travel—and how much trouble can be caused. I learned to *remove* myself when others gossiped or tore maliciously behind the backs of their victims—sneering remarks because their clothes "look funny" or "aren't name-brands," or who did and didn't sleep with boys or go to wild parties. And, I learned to *keep my mouth shut* about what I did overhear—lest I add to someone's already heavy load.

As a girl, my mother taught me to say nice things about and to people—to give compliments and encourage people—to reach out to those who feel left out. I'm grateful! I've seen the results in others — and I've seen the results in me, too. I prefer the *good* feeling of having something "kind" to say about someone, than the *yucky* feeling that hangs like a dark cloud when hurtful things are said. Whether, the person we talk about knows it or not, *we* know it—and it kills something inside.

I once heard, "*Little* people talk about other people; *average* people talk about things; and *big* people talk about ideas!" The English political philosopher and orator, Edmund Burke, said in the 1700's: "All that is necessary for the triumph of evil is for good people to do nothing." *Do something!* Make it a point to say *good* things about people. Choose to "go against the flow" of carnal chatter.

Jesus never gossiped or spread rumors. He never "threw stones"—neither the kind that can bruise the body, nor those that crush the soul. He didn't expose the weaknesses of others. When He was drawn into a slanderous situation by self-righteous men accusing a woman of immorality, He simply turned it around for ministry opportunities (cf. John 8:3-11):

To the ACCUSERS: He ignored them, leaving them squirming, "as though He heard them not." Then in a one-sentence sermon He got right to the heart of the matter—*their* evil hearts! "He that is without sin among you, let him first cast a stone at her," He said. One by one they all crept away! These were religious leaders, supposed pious men who represented God. More than once, Jesus exposed and reprimanded sinful "religious" people who covered their own sins, while arrogantly and self-righteously condemning others.

58

To the ACCUSED: He asked, "Woman, where are those thine accusers? hath no man condemned thee?" Then He set her free from her load of bondage and guilt— "Neither do I condemn thee: go and sin no more." Instead of "talking about her" or "stoning her," He who loves sinners, but hates sin, showed *forgiveness, love, acceptance, and mercy!*—setting an example of the character which He desires to develop in us.

Judge Gently

Please don't find fault with the man that limps,
    Or stumbles along the road,
Unless you have worn the shoes he wears
    Or struggled beneath his load.
There may be tacks in his shoes that hurt,
    Tho' hidden away from view,
Or the burden he bears placed on your back
    Might cause you to stumble, too.
Don't sneer at the man who's down today,
    Unless you have felt the blow
That caused his fall or felt the shame
    That only the fallen know.
You may be strong; but still the blows
    That were his, if dealt to you
In the selfsame way at the selfsame time
    Might cause you to stagger, too.
Don't be too harsh with the man that sins,
    Or pelt him with word or stone,
Unless you are sure — yes, double sure —
    That you have no sins of your own.
For you know perhaps if the tempter's voice
    Should whisper as soft to you
As it did to him when he went astray
    It might cause you to falter, too.

—Author Unknown

A headline in our local paper caught my eye: "Gossip: Once it gets rolling, it's tough to stop." The article reports that researchers have found why gossip tends to be so nasty: Negativism is in the very structure of gossip, and gossip is usually done in the absence of its target. Yes—it's so easy to say something negative behind someone's back when the facts can't be challenged!

In the same newspaper, I read of a horrendous blaze which destroyed 2,900 houses, killed 24 people, and caused an estimated $5 billion in damage. It all began with a tiny fire. So it is with sins of the tongue like gossip. Indeed, this is the very analogy the Bible uses:

> "Behold how great a matter a little fire kindleth! And the tongue is a fire, a world of iniquity: so is the tongue among our members that it defileth the whole body, and setteth on fire the course of nature; and it is set on fire of hell" (Jam. 3:5-6).

After he preached one night, a woman asked Ralph if he knew where the cigarette is mentioned in the Bible. He asked her if it was the verse in which Rebekah lighted off her camel (Gen. 24:64). This was not the one! Instead, she quoted Proverbs 16:27: "An ungodly man diggeth up evil: and *in his lips there is as a burning fire.*" However, the context indicates this reference is to sins of the tongue such as gossip, very similar to James' statement that "the tongue is a fire, a world of iniquity" (Jam. 3:6).

Who is worse?—the poor guy who made a mistake and muddied up his life—or the self-righteous busybody who spreads dirt?! How much better to turn a *distorted* interest in other people's affairs into something  constructive. Instead of talking to others about things that should be kept quiet, we can talk to *God* who knows the truth of the matter. Instead of muddying the waters, we can become a catalyst to bring about the cleansing of Christ whose love covers a multitude of sins. Instead of DEATH—we can bring LIFE!

Chapter 7

EXCUSES!

—by Ralph Woodrow

It did not begin with modern times—this practice of making excuses. It goes clear back to the book of Genesis and the first human pair. It spans the centuries and even on Judgment Day, according to Jesus, some will still offer excuses!

When "the Lord God planted a garden eastward in Eden," it must have been a beautiful place! Today, even with the curse on the land, there are beautiful gardens with flowers, shrubs, and trees in park-like settings. But these have been planted by *men*. How much more beautiful must this garden have been, for it was planted by *God!*

It was here, within this Edenic paradise, that God placed Adam and Eve. And, we should note, it was Adam and Eve—not Adam and Steve!

Here they could partake of the fruit of the various trees, but one part God retained to himself—the tree of the knowledge of good and evil. We all know the story. God asked Adam: "Hast thou eaten of the tree, whereof I commanded thee that thou shouldest not eat?" Adam's answer became a pattern for excuse making that has plagued mankind ever since. Notice how quick he was to make an excuse—shifting the blame to the woman!

"The *woman* that thou gavest to be with me, *she* gave me of the tree and I did eat" (Gen. 3:12).

Not only did Adam blame the woman, but it is almost like he blamed God also—"...the woman that *thou* gavest to be with me..." Today, people do wrong and try to blame God. But, "Let no man say when he is tempted, I am tempted of God...every man is tempted, when he is drawn away of his own lust and enticed" (Jam. 1:13,14).

When God asked Eve about the situation, her reply was: "The serpent beguiled me, and I did eat." Does this sound familiar? Still today, there are some who offer the excuse: "The Devil made me do it!"

The first thing people do when they go wrong is blame *someone else*. They blame the preacher, the teacher, the deacons, the inlaws, the outlaws! They blame their husband or wife, as the case may be. "Oh if my wife would serve God, I would serve him!" Better serve God whether she ever does or not. "If my husband would give his heart to the Lord, so would I." Better do it anyhow! Trying to put the blame on others robs us of God's best in our lives.

A better attitude is summed up in the words of a chorus from years past:

Not my brother, not my sister, but it's me O Lord,
    standing in the need of prayer;
not the deacons, not the preacher, but it's me O Lord,
    standing in the need of prayer.

"So then every one of us shall give account of *himself* to God" (Rom. 14:12).

There are some who will not attend church. They say there's a hypocrite in the church. But if there's a hypocrite standing between you and God—*he's closer to God than you are!* Think about it. We don't throw all our money away just because there are a few counterfeit bills in circulation. If there's a counterfeit, it implies there is the genuine. If there's a false, there must be a true. If there is a wrong, there must be a right.

Let me tell you about a man who spent a lot of time walking around in the desert—an expert at excuse making. One day he saw a bush that was on fire. It was not a stately oak or a majestic fir; just one of so many dust-covered bushes on the desert. But there was something different about this bush—it was on fire and not consumed. It got his attention and when he got closer, the Lord spoke out of the bush commissioning him to bring deliverance to the slaves in Egypt. But he made an excuse!

"Who am I, that I should go unto Pharaoh, and that I should bring forth the children of Israel out of Egypt?" (Ex. 3:11). Surely he should have known, witnessing the miracle of the burning bush, and hearing God's voice, that God would make a way. But he was human. And, who was he anyhow?

He no doubt remembered how 40 years before he had actually tried to be a deliverer, but failed. At that time, he defended an Israelite, and killed an Egyptian, "FOR he supposed his brethren would have understood how that God by *his* hand would deliver them: but they understood not" (Acts 7:25). Moses was ready *then* to bring deliverance; but the people did not accept him.

Being wanted for murder, he fled as a fugitive to the backside of the desert. Had there been a Post Office in Egypt, his picture would have been on the bulletin board with the "most wanted criminals." Imagine getting a call to go back to the very area where one had committed murder!

To deliver this multitude of slaves from Egypt would require a miracle ministry greater than any he had ever dared to dream of. To get his message across to these people would be no easy task, and to get them to believe in him might be even more difficult. He had been rejected before—would they accept him now? Besides he was eighty years old—they would probably figure he was senile—even hearing "voices" talking to him. At eighty he was "too old for the young people."

But even if he succeeded in getting all of these slaves out of Egypt, what then? When they would face a large

63

body of water standing in their way, there would be no Golden Gate suspension bridge or ships waiting to take them across! Those waters would need to swing open on the hinges of omnipotent power and the paths of men be laid in the depths of the sea. They would need a miracle cloud to guide them by day and a pillar of fire by night; they would need a miracle of manna from heaven and water from a rock in that desert! Who had ever dreamed of such things? There was nothing like this in the bylaws of his denomination. No wonder he said: "Who am I?"

"But who will I say sent me?" Moses asked. His credentials had long since expired! God said: "I AM THAT I AM" (Ex. 3:14). What a thrilling name! Surely, what God used to be, he is now; what he is now, he always will be—"the same yesterday, and today, and forever" (Heb. 13:8). Some are prone to think of him as the great "I used to be," as though his power was exhausted on some former generation; or they think of him as the great "I will be" in some future Heaven or Golden Age. But he is in the NOW, he is indeed the great I AM. He was God, not only of Abraham, but also of Isaac, and still later of Jacob—and now of Moses! People pass on, centuries pile on centuries, but he is the *same* (Heb. 1:12).

Moses had another excuse: "O my Lord, I am not eloquent, neither heretofore, nor since thou hast spoken unto thy servant: but I am slow of speech, and of a slow tongue" (Ex. 4:10). Because Moses was such a champion of faith, because he is so famous, we sometimes tend to forget that he was not an outstanding speaker. Being slow of speech, by natural reasoning, was a "good" excuse.

Finally, he quit making excuses. Though he was eighty years old, it was not time to "retire," it was time to "REFIRE." He who had been a nobody on the back side of the desert went from zero to hero as the Exodus became a reality!

But all was not smooth sailing even then. A few weeks later, while Moses sought God on the mountain, the people fell into idolatry in the valley below (Ex. 32). They demanded of Aaron a god they could see. Then, having made a golden calf, "they sat down to eat and to drink, and rose up to play," and in a "naked" state took part in pagan fertility rites (verses 4, 25).

When Moses returned from the mountain, with the tables of the ten commandments in his hand, he confronted Aaron, the man left in charge, about the golden calf. Aaron could not deny its existence, but notice the excuse he made:

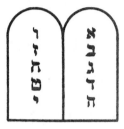

"And I said unto them, Whosoever hath any gold, let them break it off. So they gave it me: then I cast it into the fire, and *there came out this calf*"! (Exod. 32:24).

What? Aaron talks as though the golden calf was an unexplainable phenomenon! A surprise! But the fact is, he "fashioned it with a graving tool, after he had made it a molten calf" (verse 4)—*it did not just happen!*

Tabloid papers commonly feature bizarre headlines:

NOAH'S ARK FOUND IN PENNSYLVANIA!
NIXON WAS PREPARING ELVIS TO BE NEXT PRESIDENT!
NINETY-EIGHT YEAR OLD WOMAN GIVES BIRTH TO BABY WITH THREE HEADS!

Aaron's excuse, if taken seriously, would have ranked right up there with the rest of them:

THOUSANDS WITNESS INCREDIBLE CALF-LIKE CREATURE MIRACULOUSLY EMERGE FROM BURNING FIRE!

At still another period in Israel's history, the people were in bondage—and again God raised up a deliverer: Gideon. When we think of Gideon, we usually recall how he was one of those faith heros who subdued kingdoms and turned to flight the armies of the aliens (Heb. 11:32). We do not think of him as an excuse maker, but he was —at one time!

65

The Midianites had taken away their crops and possessions. They were oppressed, frustrated, and fearful—Gideon included. One day while Gideon was fearfully threshing wheat by a winepress, a man sitting under a nearby oak tree spoke to him: "The Lord is with thee, thou mighty man of valor"! (Jud. 13:12). Gideon might have said: *"Who me?"*

Gideon wanted to know something—if the Lord was with them, why were they in this trouble? Why were they not seeing miracles, as when God brought the Israelites out of Egypt? He did not realize, apparently, that a miracle was taking place then and there—that this "man" who was talking to him was actually an *angel* from the courts of God! The angel's message was that the Lord wanted Gideon to deliver the people from the Midianite bondage. At first Gideon made an excuse:

"Oh my Lord, wherewith shall I save Israel? behold, my family is poor in Manasseh, and I am the least in my father's house" (Jud. 6:15).

We might have sympathized with Gideon. If he was a nobody, if he was poor, if he had no social standing, if he was not well-known—how *would* he bring deliverance to the people? Finally he quit saying "I can't," and started saying, "I can," and the rest is now history.

The last letters in the word American are "I can." Paul put it this way: "I CAN do all things through Christ which strengtheneth me" (Phil. 4:13). "For it is GOD who worketh in you both to will and to do of his good pleasure" (Phil. 2:13). "The people that do know their God shall be strong, and do exploits" (Dan. 11:32). In ourselves we are nothing; but through *him* "we are MORE THAN CONQUERORS" (Rom. 8:37). Praise God!

God says you can; Satan says you can't. The way *you* vote makes a majority. Jesus said: "The thief comes but for to steal to kill and to destroy; I am come that you might have life and have it more abundantly" (John 10:10).

When God called Jeremiah to do a work for him, his excuse was that he was too young!

"Ah, Lord God! behold, I cannot speak: for I am a child" (Jer. 1:6).

Again, this seemed like a "good" excuse. But, nevertheless, he did speak; and became one of the most famous prophets that ever lived. His writings make up the second longest book in the Bible, having (in English, King James Version) 42,659 words, second only to the Psalms with 43,743 words.

On a personal note, I thank God that from my youth I have had the opportunity to preach the gospel of our Lord Jesus Christ, having been in his work full time since age 18! Can God use young people? Certainly. Timothy was a young preacher (1 Tim. 4:12) and even Paul—though we commonly think of him as Paul "the aged" (Philm. 9)—had his life turned around while still a "young man" (Acts 7:58).

The child Samuel heard the Lord's voice when the old man, Eli, no longer heard the voice of God (1 Sam. 2:1-10). David's older brothers were passed over and the young David became the Lord's choice (1 Sam. 16:11).

Jesus called a little child to him as an object lesson, and said: "Except you be converted, and become as little children, you shall not enter into the kingdom of heaven" (Matt. 18:3). When children were crying out words of praise, "Hosanna to the son of David," some of the Jewish priests were upset. Jesus asked them if they had never read: "Out of the mouths of babes and sucklings thou has perfected praise"? (Matt. 21:15,16). And if we want to get younger still, how about this: John the Baptist was filled with the Holy Ghost from his mother's womb! (Lk. 1:15).

It has been said that the young people are the church of tomorrow. But the young people are an important part of the church *today!* A good church reaches out to people of all ages and, ideally, will have people of all different ages— including children and young people. No one is too young or too old to be  used of God, since the outpouring of the Holy Spirit includes all—young and old, male and female, rich and poor (Acts 2:17,18).

A common excuse today is: "I'm too busy!" People claim they are too busy to pray each day, too busy to read the Bible, yet somehow they find time to do other things. A poem I first read back in the 50s (author unknown) provides some valid admonition:

> *You've time to build houses, and in them to dwell,*
> *And time to do business—to buy and to sell,*
> *But none for repentance, or deep earnest prayer,*
> *To seek your salvation you've no time to spare.*
>
> *You've time for earth's pleasures for frolic and fun,*
> *For her glittering treasures how quickly you run,*
> *But care not to seek the fair mansions above,*
> *The favor of God or the gift of his love.*
>
> *You've time to take voyages over the sea,*
> *And time to take in the world's jubilee;*
> *But soon your bright hopes will be lost in the gloom,*
> *Of the cold, dark wave of death, and the tomb.*
>
> *You've time to resort to woods, mountain and glen,*
> *And time to gain knowledge from books and of men,*
> *Yet no time to search for the wisdom of God:*
> *But what of your soul when you're under the sod?*
>
> *For time will not linger when helpless you lie,*
> *Staring death in the face, you will take time to die!*
> *Then, what of the judgment?*
> *Pause, think, I implore!*
> *For time will be lost on eternity's shore.*

In one of his parables, Jesus told of a man who prepared a great supper and invited many guests, but they all claimed to be busy with other things:

"They all with one consent began to make *excuse*. The first said unto him, I have bought a piece of ground, and I must needs go and see it: I pray thee have me excused. And another said, I have bought five yoke of oxen, and I go to prove them: I pray thee have me excused. And another said, I have married a wife, and therefore I cannot come" (Lk. 14:18-20).

One questions why a man would buy a piece of property sight unseen, but things like that do happen sometimes. Another was concerned about his purchase of cattle. The man who had just gotten married was leaving on his honeymoon! If these were true statements, they were pretty "good" excuses. But even good excuses do not change God's plan, but tend to rob us of God's best in our lives.

A man once came to Jesus and said he would follow him anywhere! He saw the miracles of Jesus, the crowds, the glamor of it all. He wanted to join the team. But when Jesus said to him: "Foxes have holes, and birds of the air have nests; but the Son of man hath not where to lay his head," we hear no more from this man! (Lk. 7:57.58). So often people want the crown, but not the cross. They like the promises, but not the commandments.

"And another also said, Lord, I will follow thee; *but...*" (Lk. 7:61). "BUT..." I heard a man years ago preach on billy goat Christians who but this and but that—constantly making statements like: "I would have been to church, but..."

Some people do not attend any church. Their excuse is that they don't agree with everything. One man said, "When I find the perfect church, I will join it!" Someone else spoke up: "Better not do that—if *you* join it, IT WILL NOT BE PERFECT ANYMORE!"

"Let us hold fast the profession of our faith...NOT forsaking the assembling of ourselves together, *as the*

69

manner of some is; but exhorting one another: and so much the more, as you see the day approaching" (Heb. 10:23-25).

Those who failed to assemble together with believers were not unsaved people, or pagans, or atheists—none of which would be expected to attend services anyhow. Those who had this "manner" or custom, were professing believers in Christ. But, probably, because of some doctrinal disagreement, they felt justified in staying home. Perhaps their excuse was that they wanted a perfect church, and not finding it, like some today, attended no church at all!

While living at Nazareth, Jesus was a *regular* at religious services. *"...as his custom was,* he went into the synagogue on the sabbath day" (Lk. 4:16). This does not imply that the synagogue was perfect or that people there understood all doctrines perfectly. Nevertheless, at Nazareth this was a center for the worship of God—and Jesus was a part of it! He didn't refuse to attend because the rabbis had less understanding than he did!

Those who make the excuse that they require a perfect church apparently forget that even the churches founded by the apostles had their faults and failures also.

At Corinth, some of the members were even denying the resurrection. Having been saved from an ungodly background, some supposed celibacy was God's requirement. There was carnality, envy, strife, and divisions —some saying, "I am of Paul," and others, "I am of Apollos." Services were disorderly and lacked structure. Gifts of the Holy Spirit, such as speaking in tongues and prophecy, were being misused and abused. Paul's writing of the "Love Chapter" implies there was weakness in this area. Their communion service had become a mere supper, with the rich having much and the poor being shamed. One of their members was involved in incest.

Quite a church! Yet—and this is our point—this was *"the* church of *God* at Corinth." Had we lived in Corinth at the time, we could have given a lot of good excuses for not attending this church! But there is not the slightest hint, biblically speaking, that this would be proper.

While the *ideal* is that we all see "eye to eye" (Isa. 51:8) and all "speak the same thing" (1 Cor. 1:10), yet the New Testament allows room for certain differences of understanding as we grow in Christ (Rom. 14). We must keep in mind that truth is vast; it is not limited to a few points of doctrine. No one person has all the truth or every divine gift. The Holy Spirit divides these to every member of the body of Christ as *he* wills (1 Cor 12:11-17). It ends up we all need each other. No man is an island. An arrogant, know-it-all attitude short-circuits the flow of God's Holy Spirit in our lives. As the Psalmist, we should pray, "Renew a right spirit within me" (Psa. 51:10).

A person who can't fit in with any church, who supposes that he *alone* has all the truth, is like the man who said: "Every one is wrong except you and me, and sometimes I wonder about thee!"

I am not saying to just attend *any* church. I am not recommending fellowship with cults and extremist groups that shame the gospel. One should seek to find a church that comes the closest to what he believes the Bible teaches, one that is being blessed by God in a community, one that is victorious and loving, one with Spirit! If there are children in the family, a church  with a good young people's group that includes such activities as summer camps, is a *must*.

The pastor of a church is in a precarious position; he can't please everyone! It has been said:

Pity the Pastor

If he is young, he lacks experience; if his hair is grey, he's too old for the young people.

If he has several children, he has too many; if he has no children, he's setting a bad example.

If he preaches from his notes, he has canned sermons and is too dry; if he doesn't use notes, he has not studied and is not deep.

If he is attentive to the poor people in the church, they claim he is playing to the grandstand; if he pays attention to the wealthy, he is trying to be an aristocrat.

If he suggests changes for improvement of the church, he is a dictator; if he makes no suggestions he is a figurehead.

If he uses too many illustrations, he neglects the Bible; if he doesn't use enough illustrations, he isn't clear.

If he condemns wrong, he's cranky; if he doesn't preach against sin, he's a compromiser.

If he preaches the truth, he's offensive; if he doesn't preach the truth, he's a hypocrite.

If he fails to please somebody, he's hurting the church and ought to leave; if he tries to please everybody, he's a fool.

If he preaches about money, he's a money grabber; if he doesn't preach scriptural giving, he is failing to develop the people.

If he drives an old car, he shames his congregation; if he drives a new car, he is setting his affection upon earthly things.

If he preaches all the time, the people get tired of hearing one man; if he invites guest speakers, he is shirking his responsibility.

If he receives a large salary, he's mercenary; if he receives only a small salary, well—it proves he isn't worth much anyway.

This is, of course, an exaggerated picture, but it makes a point. No pastor is perfect, but in spite of imperfections, *God uses pastors* to preach the gospel whereby people are saved!

Consider the following application that was received by a church that needed a pastor:

"Gentlemen: Understanding your pulpit is vacant, I should like to apply for the position. I have many qualifications. I've been a preacher with much success and also have had some success as a writer. Some say I'm a good organizer. I've been a leader most places I've been.

"I'm over 50 years of age and have never preached in one place for more than three years. In some places, I have left town after my work caused riots and disturbances. I must admit I have been in jail three or four times, but not because of any real wrongdoing.

"My health is not too good, though I still accomplish a great deal. The churches I have preached in have been small, though located in several large cities.

"I've not gotten along well with religious leaders in the towns where I have preached. In fact, some have threatened me, and even attacked me physically. I am not too good at keeping records. I have been known to forget whom I have baptized.

"However, if you can use me, I promise to do my best for you."

The good church folks were appalled! Consider a sickly, trouble-making, absent-minded ex-jailbird? Never! Then someone looked to see who this nervy person was who had written the letter. It was signed, "The Apostle Paul."

People have offered all kinds of excuses. Some who are not serving the Lord make the excuse that they do not understand God or the Bible. Well, I don't understand how a brown cow, who sleeps in a red barn, and eats green grass, can produce white milk and yellow butter! But it happens.

73

To receive salvation does not require that we understand God or everything about his word. The Bible says, "Abraham *believed* God"—it does not say he *understood* God—"and it was counted unto him for righteousness" (Rom. 4:3).

The practice of excuse making began back with Adam and Eve. We have seen it throughout biblical history. We all know it is a common practice today. Ironically, it will not stop with human history, but even clear down at Judgment Day some will even dare to make excuses! We have this on the authority of Jesus himself that many will come on that Day and claim to have done wonderful works, yet to whom he will say: "I never knew you: depart from me, you that work iniquity" (Matt. 7:21-23).

How much better to hear the words: "Well done, good and faithful servant...enter into the joy of thy Lord" (Matt. 25:21)!

A Round Tuit

At long last, here is a Round Tuit. Guard it with your life and never lose it. These tuits have been hard to come by, especially the round ones. They are indispensable for Christians, for if properly used can be very helpful. For years we have heard people say, "I'll do this as soon as I get 'a round tuit'." Now that you have 'a round tuit' many things that have been needing to be accomplished will get done forthwith.

Chapter 8

DIVINE LOVE

—by Ralph Woodrow

The word "love" carries different meanings to different people. There is sweetheart love, a mother's love for her child, love for humanity, etc.
But God's love is far more lasting and deeper than any of these. It is more than mere "puppy love"— puppy love might lead you a dog's life! The love of which we are speaking is *divine love*—the love that is shed abroad in our hearts by the Holy Spirit (Rom. 5:5).

God's love for man comes through clearly in the golden text of the Bible, John 3:16: "God *so loved* the world, that he gave his only begotten Son, that whosoever believeth in him should not perish, but have everlasting life." In another passage, the wording is similar: "In this was manifested the *love* of God toward us, because that God sent his only begotten Son into the world, that we might live through him....Beloved, if God *so loved* us, we ought also to *love* one another" (1 John 4:9-11).

Jesus said, "By this shall all men know that ye are my disciples, if ye have LOVE one to another" (John 13:35). Jesus did not say that all men would recognize his disciples because they went by a certain name, met in a certain kind of building, or because they had headquarters in a certain place. Jesus did not say that all men would recognize his disciples because they ascribed to a certain set of doctrines, for the world in general knows little about fine points of doctrine. But by demonstrating a life of love—divine love—the true people of God can be identified. The language of love transcends all language barriers!

Not only is this love a sign to the world of our discipleship, it is a witness in our own hearts that we are Christians! "We know that we have passed from death unto life, because we LOVE the brethren" (1 John 3:14). Do you wonder if you are really a Christian? If you are, you will love the brethren.

Without this love, we are liars and murderers in the sight of God! "If a man says, I love God, and hates his brother, he is a *liar:* for he that loves not his brother whom he has seen, how can he love God whom he has not seen?" (1 John 4:20). In no uncertain terms, the Bible says: "Whosoever hates his brother is a *murderer:* and you know that no murderer has eternal life abiding in him" (1 John 3:15). Strong words!

The man who does not have love, certainly does not have God's Spirit, for "God is *love*" (1 John 4:16). The Spirit of God will cause us to love the brethren—all who have repented of their sins and turned to Jesus Christ. They may not all see everything about the plan of God just alike, but this does not change the fact they are brethren.

Suppose two brothers were discussing mathematics—one a college student, the other a fifth grader. How foolish it would be for the college student to argue with his younger brother about geometry! Certainly they would not understand mathematics the same. Still they are brothers! So is it within the family of God. There are different levels of understanding. Some are "babes" in Christ, while others are more mature (1 Pet. 2:2; Heb. 5:13,14). If some truth has come to us, a truth that our brother does not yet see, we should be humble and loving, bearing in mind that "knowledge puffeth up, but love edifieth" (1 Cor. 8:1).

If we feel our brother is wrong on some point, we will never change him for the better by hatred. If we must disagree on something, let us not be *disagreeable*. People are won by love, not by trying to force them to believe a certain way. This truth might well be illustrated by the children's story of *The Sun and the Wind.*

The Sun and the Wind discussed which of them was the strongest. The Wind said he could prove he was the strongest by blowing the coat off a man who walked on the road below. So the Sun slipped behind a cloud and Mr. Wind started blowing until the man thought a tornado

had come up! But the harder the Wind blew, the tighter the man held onto his coat. Finally the Wind saw that he could not blow the man's coat off, so he gave up in defeat.

Then it was the Sun's turn to try. As Mr. Sun came out from behind the clouds, he smiled kindly on the man. Presently the warm loving rays of the Sun caused the man to pull off his coat. The Sun had proved that the power of love and kindness is stronger than fury and force!

77

I once saw two preachers discussing—well, really, *arguing*—about the "Rapture"! To a bystander it would appear they were really getting worked up about it. One was "Pre-Trib," the other was "Post-Trib"—each accusing the other of being *wrong!* Which one do *I* think was wrong? I think they were *both* wrong—wrong in that they allowed a doctrinal difference to mar their love for one another as brothers in Christ!

This is not to say that we should not study out a matter; this is not to say we should not take a stand for truth as we come to see it in the scriptures; but we must "speak the truth in *love*" (Eph. 4:15). Our *priorities* must be right.

The love of God causes us to be willing to *accept* one another. Without this love, we tend to *reject* one another—sometimes over minor differences. Among brethren, is our attitude such that we think in terms of the *many* things we agree on?—or does our attitude cause us to zero in on the *few* things on which we differ? The emphasis should be on *cooperation,* not *competition.* Our ship should be The Fellowship, not The Battleship.

"Variance" is listed by Paul as a work of the flesh, contrary to "love" which is a fruit of the Spirit (Gal. 5:19-23). Have you ever known people who practice *variance*? No matter what someone says, they seem to have a different opinion. One person might say an item cost $2.98. The other will interrupt, saying it cost $2.88, even though this minor difference is not essential to the overall story! Some people seem to "enjoy" correcting others, even though the correction serves no real purpose. Variance causes people to be different and difficult.

Sometimes we are prone to criticize highly visible ministries, such as Christian television programs. They're too emotional or not emotional enough. They're too flamboyant in programming or personal grooming. We may not see eye-to-eye on certain doctrinal issues or we sense a prideful arrogance. Some criticism may be justified. But even in Paul's day, not everyone who preached Christ did so with the best motives. Yet, notice how he handled it:

"Some preach Christ even of envy and strife, and some of good will: the one preach Christ of contention, not sincerely...but the other of *love*...What then? notwithstanding, every way, whether in pretense, or in truth, CHRIST IS PREACHED; and I therein do rejoice, yea, and will rejoice" (Phil. 1:15-18).

And so it is today. Christ is being preached. It is God's work, his church, and his business to ultimately judge or justify. He will sort it all out. It is our business to love and build up our fellow Christians—not to hate and tear down! Those who continually run down others usually have something wrong in their own lives.

Some people are like a woman who used to look out her window at her neighbor's wash hanging on the line. Each week she would say, "My! those sheets look so dirty. That woman never gets her wash clean!" But one day she washed *her own windows.* Next Monday, the neighbor's wash looked perfectly white! All she needed to do was wash her own windows!

Jesus, using what has been described as "high voltage vocabulary," spoke of the hypocrisy of one trying to pull the "mote" out of his brother's eye, when he had a "beam" in his own (Matt. 7:3-5). Put in modern terms, the question might be: "Why do you try to take a speck of *sawdust* out of your brother's eye, when you have a *telephone pole* in your own?"

The love message is strong meat. It is not a watered down, sugarcoated message. It puts demands on us. So intense should be our love for the brethren, that as Christ "laid down his life for us...we ought to *lay down our lives for the brethren*" (1 John 3:16). But instead of this, sadly, some will allow the least little thing to turn people against each other.

Some people love the "brethren" as long as they belong to the same denomination. But in some cases— sometimes right in the same denomination and local assembly—people will lose their love for the brethren. Churches have split over such petty things as who is going to play the piano—or even if they should have a piano!

I know of a group that believed in taking the Lord's supper and washing feet once a year—at passover time— but split because they could not agree on which came first. Should they wash feet first, then take the Lord's supper— or take the Lord's supper first, then wash feet? The whole issue hinged on an interpretation of the phrase: "And supper being ended [finished]" (John 13:2). Did this mean supper was finished, so that they were now ready to eat; or did it mean they were finished with supper?

A pastor once told me he was facing a serious problem in his church. They had built a lovely house of worship. They were going to decide on what color they wanted for the seats. They had two types of fabric from which to choose—one a pale red, the other green. It seems about half wanted red, the other half wanted green. Neither side would give in. The pastor told me it was about to split his church!

The story is told of one church that even split on a hair! That's a pretty fine line to split on, isn't it? Apparently different ladies in the church baked cakes for a young visiting preacher. Later he thanked them for the cakes, but added that one cake had a long hair in

it. Each of the ladies was sure it wasn't her cake. Some thought it was probably Sister Smith's cake and others felt it was Sister Jones' cake. Finally people took sides and, according to the story, the church split over the issue—split on a hair!

Notice the emphasis the scriptures place on love. Peter wrote: "And *above all things* have fervent charity [love] among yourselves; for charity [love] shall cover the multitude of sins" (1 Pet. 4:8,9). Paul admonished Christians to show "kindness, humbleness of mind, meekness, long-suffering; forbearing one another, and forgiving one another. If any man have a quarrel against any: even as Christ forgave you, so also do ye. And *above all these things* put on charity [love] which is the bond of perfectness" (Col. 3:12-14).

If one is able to help those in need, and refuses, "how dwelleth the love of God in him? My little children, let us not love in word, neither in tongue: but in deed and in truth" (1 John 3:17,18).

Some folks are like a lady who stood in church and testified, "I love everybody I *see*," but she had her eyes shut the whole time!

How many commandments were there in the law? Certainly there were more than ten! Jewish rabbis spoke of 613 commandments. It was sometimes debated which was the least and which was the greatest. When Jesus was asked which was the great commandment in the law, his reply was this: "Thou shalt *love* the Lord thy God with all thy heart, and with all thy soul, and with all thy mind"—a quotation from Deuteronomy 6:5. "This," Jesus explained, "is the first and great commandment. And the second is like unto it, Thou shalt *love* thy neighbor as thyself"—a quotation from Leviticus 19:18. (Interestingly, these two great commandments which Jesus cited were not quoted from the Ten Commandments.) Jesus continued: "On these two commandments hang all the law and the prophets" (Matt. 22:35-46). In other words, the basis of God's entire program is love!

The true love of God will even cause us to love our ENEMIES. Jesus said: "Love your enemies, bless them that curse you, do good to them that hate you, and pray for them which despitefully use you, and persecute you" (Matt. 5:43-48). When a person can truly, honestly, sincerely, have love even for his enemies, he indeed has the love of God in his heart!

Some people become hateful and angry over even little things. But the Bible says, "Let all bitterness, and wrath, and anger, and clamor, and evil speaking, be put away from you, with all malice: and be ye kind one to another, tenderhearted, forgiving one another, even as God for  Christ's sake hath forgiven you" (Eph. 4:31,32). The Bible repeatedly stresses such things as forgiveness, kindness, mercy, and tenderness—qualities that are often lost in a maze of doctrines and religious dogmas.

If we have the love of God, we will not make fun of others because of some problem they have. How often children at school will make fun of others because they are "fat" or "skinny," because of the color of their skin, or if they stutter, or have a deformity or because they are poor. Such "fun" is cruel and hateful. Older people—though usually in more sophisticated ways—often show the same lack of consideration.

If we have Christian love, we will not only be kind to people, but also to animals. I have often pointed this out—it is a "pet doctrine" with me. I have known of people who try to run over a dog if it runs out at their car—and then laugh about hitting it as they speed on down the road. Apparently they don't care that the dog may have been some little child's pet whose heart will be broken because of such cruelty.

I once read in the newspaper about a woman who was walking her dog along a canal. The dog ran on ahead to where a group of youngsters were playing. They grabbed the little dog and drowned it—before the woman could get there. Then they ran off laughing. Such cruelty shows how badly this world needs the LOVE of God!

Some will not properly feed or care for their animals. Even the Bible makes provision for the oxen that tread out the corn. An ox is not to be muzzled—he is to be left free to eat while he is working (1 Tim. 5:18). "A good man is concerned for the welfare of his animals" (Pro. 12:10, Living Bible).

Years ago, there was a comedy movie *Francis the Talking Mule*. Later, a television series featured "Mr. Ed," a talking horse. But long before either of these, in the Bible, we have the case of Baalam's donkey who was actually given the power of human speech—long enough to ask the wayward prophet why he was treating him unkindly! (Num. 22:28).

I believe that love can and must be practiced in business dealings. Suppose we have a car to sell and the prospective buyer asks if the car is in good condition. If we know the transmission is about to go out, that the car burns oil, that it has a cracked block, etc., we are liars if we say it is in good condition. Yet, there are those who would do this and still profess to have love. They can't have love and be so selfish. We might fool people and make a sale, but we can never fool God!

A Christian can even dem-
onstrate the love of God in the
way he drives on the highway.
He can drive with kindness and
courtesy. A minister friend of
mine told me about a man who
saw a bumper sticker on the car
in front of him that said: "Honk
if you love Jesus!" As he passed 
him, he honked. The man looked at him and gave him an obscene finger gesture!

Some who go to buy a product will run it down, down, down, to the man who is selling it (without any real reason for doing so) until they buy it for little or nothing—then go brag about it to others: "It is naught, it is naught, saith the buyer: but when he is gone his way, then he boasteth" (Pro. 20:14). Such two-faced hypocrisy is certainly not divine love!

Paul wrote: "Husbands, love your wives" (Eph. 5:25). Now the fact that he wrote these words clearly implies there was a *need* for this admonition. Some husbands were not loving toward their wives, were not treating them right. A couple who had been married for quite a few years went to a pastor for counselling. The wife felt her husband didn't love her. "Have you ever told your wife you love her?"

84

the pastor asked. "Yep," the man replied, "when me and the Mrs. got married, I told her then—it still holds!" Couples should not hesitate to say it: "I love you."

A story is told of a pastor who was so busy serving the church, he paid little attention to his wife. She became depressed and he took her to a doctor. The doctor asked her: "When was the last time your husband gave you a big hug?"

"About a year ago."

"When was the last time he kissed you?"

"About a year and a half ago."

With this the doctor grabbed her, leaned her back, and gave her a great big hug and kiss. He then turned to the husband and said: "She needs this *every day!*"

The pastor replied, "Doc, I'm a busy man. I have a tight schedule. But I guess I could bring her in on Tuesdays and Thursdays!"

Finally, the message of divine love can all be summed up in the words of Paul: "Though I speak with the tongues of men and of angels, and have not love, I am become as sounding brass or a tinkling cymbal. And though I have the gift of prophecy, and understand all mysteries, and all knowledge; and though I have all faith, so that I could remove mountains, and have not love I AM NOTHING" (1 Cor. 13:1,2).

"Love is very patient, very kind. Love knows no jealousy; love makes no parade, gives itself no airs, is never rude, never selfish, never irritated, never resentful; love is never glad when others go wrong, love is gladdened by goodness, always slow to expose, always eager to believe the best, always hopeful, always patient" (1 Cor. 13:4-7, Moffatt translation).

"Let brotherly love continue" (Heb. 13:1).

Chapter 9

FREEDOM FROM FEAR

—by Ralph Woodrow

"God has not given us the spirit of FEAR" (2 Tim. 1:7).

"FEAR has torment" (1 Jn. 4:18).

"God is love...perfect love casts out FEAR" (1 Jn. 4:16,18).

Timothy, a young preacher, had apparently allowed fear to hinder his ministry. Consequently, when Paul wrote to him, he encouraged him to "stir up the gift of God"—not to let fear hold him back—"FOR God has not given us the spirit of fear."

If our motives are right, we should never let fear stand in our way. Some never try to do anything for God, because they are afraid they will fail. But if they don't try, they have FAILED ALREADY! They are like the man Jesus mentioned who sought to justify his inaction by saying, "I was afraid" (Mt. 25:25). Fear brings defeat instead of victory, failure instead of success, tragedy instead of triumph. God has not given us this spirit.

Jesus repeatedly taught that we should not fear, should not worry, should not be of a fearful mind. His message was *for* FAITH and *against* FEAR. Yet, tragically, we see many followers of Jesus today who are troubled with fear. This should not be!

Many things that people worry about are things that will never happen—superstitious fears. One night when I was a boy, probably about five years of age, I was putting a picture puzzle together. It was a picture of a dog who had undone a ball of yarn. While working on this puzzle, a house up the street from us caught on fire. I remember the bright lights of the fire trucks, the crowd that gathered, and the flames shooting up into the sky! It ended up, the damage to the house was not too great, no one was hurt, and it was soon repaired. But to a child, the scene that night was frightening. A seed of fear was planted in my mind. For some reason, *I never wanted to put that particular puzzle together again!*

Did I suppose there was a connection? Did I think that if I worked that puzzle again another fire might start, that possibly it would be our house this time? Of course this was only a childhood experience, but even as adults, do we not also sometimes harbor unnecessary fears?

Superstition dies hard. Some still fear bad luck if they break a mirror, especially if it happens on Friday the 13th! Some high-rise buildings will omit floor 13; that is, the floors are numbered up to 12, then the next is 14, etc. Some people simply would not feel comfortable in an apartment or office on floor number 13! Sometimes hospitals will not have  a room 13. Others, while they know certain things are only superstition, still would not want to walk under a ladder or have a black cat cross their path—just in case!

But even in things more serious—I am not saying there are not *real* problems in life!—God can give peace in the place of fear. The Psalmist wrote: "God is our refuge and strength, a very present help in trouble. Therefore will not we FEAR, though the earth by removed, and though the mountains be carried into the midst of the sea...There is a river, the streams whereof shall make glad the city of God" (Ps. 46:1,2). A similar thought has been expressed in a spiritual by Doris Akers,

This old world may toss and tumble;
This old world my rock and roll.
The sun above may turn to ashes
And all fury may unfold,
Every star may fall form heaven,
And the earth may take a stroll,
But the Lord will never leave me,
He's the lover of my soul!

Or, as Stuart Hamblin expressed it in one of his songs,

Should the sun and the moon in time flicker and die,
And the earth wander off like a tramp through the sky,
The darkness can't hide me, He'll find me I know,
For men are his diamonds and he loves me so.

Hebrews 13:5,6 says: "...for he has said, I will never leave you, nor forsake you. So that we may boldly say, The Lord is my helper, and I will not FEAR what man shall do unto me." Even in the "valley of the shadow of death," he has promised to be with us, and even there we shall "FEAR no evil" (Ps. 23). "In all these things we are MORE THAN CONQUERORS through him" (Rom. 8:37).

The accompanying photograph (used by permission) is an aerial view of the south side of the famous Winchester Mystery House, in San Jose, California. A fortune had come to Mrs. Sarah Winchester—royalties of $1,000 a day—from her husband's firearms company. For 38 years she kept crews working day and night, adding on to her house—more rooms, secret passages, and trap doors! One cupboard door opens to a storage space of one-half inch, while the closet door directly across from it opens to the back 30 rooms of the sprawling house! Several stairways lead nowhere. There are hundreds of doors, 47 fireplaces, 52 skylights, and over 10,000 windows!

Why did Mrs. Winchester keep building? Because of FEAR. Fearful that the spirits of Indians and others who were killed by the Winchester guns, would kill her, she sought help from a spiritualist medium. She was told

that as long as there was the sound of hammers and construction continued on her house, she would not die! The Bible speaks of some who because of "FEAR of death" spend their whole lifetime in *bondage* (Heb. 2:15).

Often one worry leads to another. What if this were to happen?—and if this happened, then what about that?—and if that happened... It is an endless curse. Perhaps you have heard the slogan: "Why worry when you can pray?" Some have turned this around: "Why pray when you can worry?" It is reverse psychology, but it makes a point. The point is that *worry does no good.* Sometimes, in fact, the worry becomes more trau-

matic than the problem itself. In a famous speech, Franklin D. Roosevelt said: "The only thing we have to fear is FEAR itself."

The words of Job have been often quoted: "For the thing which I greatly *feared* is come upon me" (Job 3:25). Job had a fear of certain things—and they happened to him. But this is not *always* the case. There have been millions of people who have feared things that never happened to them! Many go through life with fear of a dread disease—and never get it. Others live in fear that they will get in a car wreck—and never do. What good does this worrying do? Most things people worry about never happen! This very fact may help us not to worry so much! And, if something *is* going to happen, it will happen whether we worry about it or not, so why worry?

There is a difference between concern and worry. If there is a problem, and concern about this problem causes us to face it and deal with it, this is good. If it is something we cannot solve, we should recognize this fact, put it in God's hands, and be at peace. Worry will not help anything. Keep in mind the words of what has been called the Prayer of Serenity:

> **God grant me the serenity to accept the things I cannot change, courage to change the things I can, and the wisdom to know the difference.**

I remember a woman and her daughter who came up to talk to me after I spoke at a meeting back in the 60s. The woman was probably in her 50's and her daughter who lived with her was perhaps 30. They asked if I would come to their house as they had something very important and confidential they wanted to talk to me about. Also, I was told to come to the *back* door—not the front—a request which sounded rather strange.

A few days later when I went to their house, I discovered the reason. This woman and her daughter were living in a couple rooms at the back of their large old house. The front of the house was empty, the yard unkept. They did not want people to know that anyone was living there. The windows of the two rooms they lived in were covered with burlap. At nights only a dim light, if any, was used. Why the would-be disguise? Why the strange and uncomfortable living conditions? These poor women imagined the COMMUNISTS were after them; that the COMMUNISTS were trying to *murder* them. Fear, especially in the mother, had become a mental obsession. "Fear has *torment*" (1 Jn. 4:18).

In his book *The Power of Positive Thinking,* Norman Vincent Peale wrote that negative ideas should be eliminated from conversations. If you are with a group of people at a luncheon, he said, do not comment that the "Communists will soon take over the country," for in the first place, Communists are not going to take over the country and by saying things such as this, one only creates a depressing reaction in the minds of others.

Some people become fearful around election time. I heard a preacher say in 1960 that if John F. Kennedy won the election, within six months he would have every Bible-believing church closed up! When Kennedy won the election, this man had a heart attack and almost died! I knew some lovely people who campaigned "For God and Goldwater." They believed that if Goldwater lost the election to Lyndon Johnson, the tribulation would be upon us! Fear caused them to sell their home and move into a very remote area. Their lives would have been better, happier, and more productive if they had stayed right where they were.

Too often people become alarmed about what this world leader or that is going to do. But we should remember that when Pilate said to Jesus: "Do you not know that I have power to crucify you, and have power to release you?" Jesus answered: "You could have no power at all against me, except it were given you FROM ABOVE"

(John 19:10,11). I still believe it is GOD who makes and unmakes nations!

There are gloom and doom preachers who specialize in preaching fear more than faith. They suppose they must always tell the bad side of things. If they mention the president, it is only to criticize. When they speak of America, it is almost always what is wrong—not what is right—with America. They talk about the problems, about how bad things are, about the shortcomings, but seldom suggest practical answers. How can they? Their whole religious outlook is that everything will get worse and worse anyhow, nothing will turn out right.

With each new election or change (in this changing world), they suspect a vast conspiracy. They live on the banks of Armageddon—and apparently feel they should preach fear all the time so they will have company. No wonder people don't want to go to church and hear long-winded sermons that are totally negative. I don't blame them! People have enough problems on the job, in the home, in the everyday activities of life. A church service ought to build them UP, not push them DOWN; should HELP, not HINDER them; should be based on FAITH, not FEAR!

I am not saying there are no problems or troubles in the world. But I think it is a question of where the *emphasis* should be placed. Paul said to think on things that are pure, lovely, and of good report. "And the PEACE of God, which passes all understanding, shall keep your hearts and minds through Christ Jesus" (Phil. 4:7,8).

Fear is not of God. Why allow superstitious fears to rob and hinder your outlook on life? Why not commit your way unto the Lord? Jesus has promised us peace, even his peace, and tells us not to be afraid. "PEACE I leave with you. MY peace I give unto you...Let not your heart be troubled, neither let it be AFRAID" (John 14:27).

Chapter 10

Let Us Be Ignited By The F.L.A.M.E. That Ignites Life

—by Arlene Woodrow

The Christian message spread around the world like wildfire nearly 2,000 years ago. At times the blaze has nearly died out in spite of powerful religious institutions. At other times a flickering ember of revival has burst forth like a raging prairie fire.

Why does the fire burn brighter or nearly die out? What brings and sustains revival fire?

The answer to keeping the fire ablaze can be found in the life and ministry of Jesus. His entire ministry is embodied in one word—COMPASSION. His compassion is all encompassing, revealing key characteristics that have been evident in lives throughout history in every outbreak of revival fire.

COMPASSION is defined as a deep feeling of sharing the suffering of another; to sympathize; to care for, be concerned or interested in another as the object of one's attention. The basic qualities of Jesus' compassionate character and ministry form the following acrostic:

Forgiveness

Love

Acceptance

Mercy

Evangelism

93

Jesus could exemplify these qualities of His character in all circumstances because:

- He was full of the power of God.
- He relied heavily on the Source of His power for strength and direction—spending much time in communion and fellowship with His Heavenly Father.
- He knew who He was and was not threatened by the evil of others.
- He cared more for others than for Himself.
- His motives were pure.
- He was convinced of the reality of the LIGHT and LIFE of the Kingdom of God vs. the DARKNESS and DEATH of the kingdom of darkness.
- He was sure of His mission.

Though Jesus was the *sinless one,* ironically He submitted Himself to the baptism of *repentance.* The regime of the kingdom of darkness was about to be overthrown—thus it was necessary for Him to represent us *"to fulfill all righteousness"* as the Kingdom of God was about to be established (cf. Mt. 3:15). Hatred, resentment, bitterness, criticism, partiality, lying, cheating, stealing, gossiping, malice, adultery, blasphemy, witchcraft, and sin of all kinds were in vogue in the kingdom of darkness (Mt. 3:2-6). But a new regime was about to overcome the darkness—and the law of the *new Kingdom of LIGHT* was to be LOVE. Jesus defined His mission of compassion at the onset of His ministry as He taught in the Synagogue, reading from the book of Isaiah (cf. Isa. 61:1-3). He said, *"This day is this scripture fulfilled in your ears":*

> *"The Spirit of the Lord is upon me, because he hath anointed me to preach the gospel to the poor; he hath sent me to heal the brokenhearted, to preach deliverance to the captives, and recovering of sight to the blind, to set at liberty them that are bruised, to preach the acceptable year of the Lord. And he closed the book, and he gave it again to the minister, and sat down. And the eyes of all them that were in the synagogue were fastened on him"* (Lk. 4:18-21 KJV).

94

In this pronouncement, we see Christ's compassionate nature. He did not come to pronounce judgment or condemnation (Jn. 3:16-21), but rather to compassionately rescue us from the clutches of evil and ruin. Everything He did was indicative of His compassionate nature.

As *we* spend time with God—on our knees and in the Word—we will become like Him as we become motivated by the Spirit that empowered Him! This spiritual investment is imperative, if we are to spread the F.L.A.M.E. to the next generations (if the Lord should tarry).

In the world there is wickedness, lawlessness, moral corruption and evil of all kinds (cf. Rom. 1:18-32). However, all is not bad news! *True revival is spontaneous*—spreading through families, communities—as well as ethnic, social, and age barriers. Let us consider the FLAME that spread across the centuries from the life and ministry of our compassionate Lord Jesus and His followers. We, too, can spread the light of this FLAME if we lay aside our self-centeredness and get really serious with God! We are *commanded* to *minister* to others through His compassionate nature:

> *"If you have any **encouragement** from being united with Christ, if any **comfort** from **his love**, if any **fellowship** with the Spirit, if any **tenderness** and **compassion**, then make my joy complete by being **like-minded**, having the **same love**, being **one in spirit and purpose**"* (Phil. 2:1-2 NIV).

The phrase *"tenderness and compassion"* above—is translated *"bowels and mercies"* in the KJV, speaking of a deep compassionate caring from the innermost self. Christians are to have intense care and deep sympathy for one another. Paul wrote, *"Therefore, as God's chosen people, holy and dearly loved, **clothe yourselves** with **COMPASSION**, **kindness**, **humility**, **gentleness** and **patience**"* (Col. 3:12 NIV).

Like Jesus, we are to minister with *compassion* and *humility*—offering *forgiveness*, *love*, *acceptance*, and *mercy*

95

to a needy world. Looking at the word "minister" etymologically (i.e., study of origin/background of words), we see that to *minister* is to **serve;** allied to **minor**—small or less. Sometimes ministers are thought of as *exalted* persons who shouldn't dirty themselves with the mundane, the downcast, the sinful. That is a *misnomer!*

"Caring" ministry is not only for those who are ministers by vocation—*all* who follow Christ are *ministers* who can and should make a difference in the world about them. That kind of ministry will naturally result in an accelerated spread of the flame of the Gospel which once burned brightly! Let us take a closer look at Jesus' compassion in action.

Jesus was motivated by compassion (Mk. 6: 34) and He truly CARED for people. He gave His life, suffered injustice and insult, loved and forgave—because of His compassion for mankind. *"When he saw the crowds, he had compassion on them, because they were harassed and helpless, like sheep without a shepherd. Then he said to his disciples, 'The harvest is plentiful but the workers are few.'"* (Mt. 9:36-37 NIV).

Later, Jesus said, *"I tell you the truth,* **anyone who has faith in me will do what I have been doing. He will do even greater things** *than these, because I am going to the Father. And* **I will do whatever you ask in my name, so that the Son may bring glory to the Father"** (Jn. 14:12-14 NIV).

Unlike *pity*, which responds with "My, my! What a shame!"—but does nothing—**compassion** responds to the need by getting *involved,* by *doing* something to alleviate the pain and to raise the hurting one to a higher plane—to show *empathy.* Empathy is defined as the action of understanding, being aware of, being sensitive to, and vicariously experiencing the feelings, thoughts, and experience of another—fully communicating in an objectively explicit manner. For instance, when Jesus

96

saw the grief of Mary and Martha whose brother, Lazarus, had died, we see His compassionate empathy—*"Jesus wept"* (Jn. 11:35). Even though Jesus knew that Lazarus was about to be resurrected, He *empathized* with the present pain and grief of his bereaved sisters. Our compassionate Savior is *"touched with the feeling of our infirmities...therefore come boldly unto the throne of grace, that we may obtain mercy, and find grace to help in time of need"* (Heb. 4:14-16).

Jesus' compassion brought *action* to the meeting of needs—relieving of hurts and injustices in day-to-day life. He *"was moved with compassion toward them, and he healed their sick"* (Mt. 14:14). Another day, *"Jesus called his disciples to him and said, 'I have compassion for these people; they have already been with me three days and have nothing to eat. I do not want to send them away hungry, or they may collapse on the way'"* (Mt. 15:32 NIV, cf. vs. 29-39). His compassion inspired Him to miraculously feed thousands!

Throughout the Gospels we see Jesus *moved with compassion* to meet the needs of the people—whether the needs were spiritual, physical, temporal, mental, or emotional. No need was too insignificant or too enormous. He not only met their needs—but He FELT their needs. His innermost being was wrenched with the sorrows of those who pressed in about Him. Peter summarized Christ's compassionate nature when he wrote, *"Cast all your anxiety on Him, because HE CARES FOR YOU"* (I Pet. 5:7 NIV).

Jesus gave His all to those around Him, and also yearned to minister to the multiplied thousands who had no one to care for them. For instance, after the Samaritan woman experienced Jesus' compassionate touch, she went to tell the people in town. They followed her, wanting to see and hear this compassionate one for themselves. While she was away telling her neighbors, Jesus shared His burden with His disciples, *"Say not ye, There*

97

are yet four months, and then cometh harvest? behold, I say unto you, Lift up your eyes, and look on the fields; for they are white already to harvest....One soweth, and another reapeth. I sent you to reap that whereon ye bestowed no labor; other men labored, and ye are entered into their labors" (Jn. 4:35-38).

Once we truly comprehend the compassion that motivated Jesus' life-changing and revolutionary ministry, we are able to understand how the Gospel sparked a fire that spread around the world and through the centuries. It is like a fire pent up within each believer (cf. Jer. 20:9)—that must warm the hearts of others—an urgency to share the light!

THE ETERNAL F.L.A.M.E. THAT BRINGS LIFE

Jesus' benevolent compassion went beyond meeting the needs of those who *deserved* His kindness. He poured His life out to sinners, his enemies, the undesirable, and the down-and-out! No persecution, rejection, or personal pain could stop Him. The compassion of Jesus is reflected in five facets of His life-giving and life-changing ministry—i.e., Forgiveness, Love, Acceptance, Mercy and Evangelism. The F.L.A.M.E. that refused to be put out by the actions of others is as follows:

FORGIVENESS is *basic* to Jesus Christ's compassionate nature. On the cross He cried out, *"Father, forgive them, for they know not what they do"* (Lk. 23:34). He didn't hold grudges. His forgiving nature allowed Him to be *all He could be,* because He was neither intimidated nor discouraged by their attacks, slander or rejection.

Peter denied Him at the moment Jesus needed Him most—when rejection, attacks, and pain were the greatest He had ever suffered. Yet, Jesus *forgave* and *restored* Peter, making him a leader in the early Church. Peter

98

received *no lecture.* Jesus didn't say, "I told you so!—I *knew* you would deny me thrice before the rooster crowed!" (cf. Mt. 26:34-35, 69-75). Our compassionate Lord just *forgave!* Peter had "blown it" so bad that he may not have *felt* forgiven at first, but Jesus tenderly asked Him a question three times that would *prove* his allegiance. Jesus asked, *"Do you love me, Peter?"* He responded, *"Lord you know I love you."* Peter's answers brought forth Jesus' statement revealing the confidence that he had for this heretofore fickle disciple: *"Feed my sheep.... Follow me"* (Jn. 21:15-17).

As humans, we would not choose someone to carry out our work who has proven unreliable in the past—but our compassionate Lord commissions His leaders from a *higher* plane. What an example of His life-giving forgiveness! He was committed to *complete* the work in Peter that He had begun—to *enable* him to effectively feed the sheep (cf. Phil. 1:6).

Peter's triple denial of his Master must have made him feel so inadequate. But, Jesus made it easy for him to turn it around. He didn't require penance or "time out"—He forgave! God's grace is sufficient to strengthen us where we are weak (cf. II Cor. 12:9).

Our compassionate Savior is not "uptight" if we fail along the way. *"He will rejoice over you with joy; He will rest [in silent satisfaction] and in His love He will be silent and make no mention [of past sins, or even recall them]; He will exult over you with singing"* (Zeph. 3:17 Amp. Bible). The Lord is not worried that we may not be able to be all that He has asked of us—He just rests and relaxes in the knowledge that His love will bring us through to perfection. That is true forgiveness in action!

Jesus forgave those whose sins were "many" (Lk. 7:47). Even Paul, who considered himself a "chief" among sinners—because he had persecuted those who believed in Christ—obtained forgiveness (1 Tim. 1:13-15). Jesus stopped him in his tracks and turned him the opposite direction! (cf. Acts 26:9-18; Gal 1:13-24). God does allow U-turns! When Jesus forgives, the guilty person starts over with a completely clean slate! If we are true followers of Christ, we too, must learn to do this kind of forgiving.

In our generation we have witnessed Dave Wilkerson (of Teen Challenge renown) exercise that kind of redeeming forgiveness on the streets of New York. Out of his ministry to drug addicts, thugs, pimps, prostitutes, and Christ-haters have come many who, having experienced the forgiveness of Christ, are in the ministry today. Though he initially suffered persecution and insults from many of them, he was willing, like Jesus, to thoroughly forgive. As they were forgiven and grew in Christ, he was able to trust them in places of leadership. That is true forgiveness in action!

Our forgiving of others is *basic* to *our* receiving forgiveness from God (Mt. 6:12, 14; Lk. 6:37). In the Lord's prayer we are taught to ask the Lord to forgive our offenses as we forgive the offenses of others. In fact, Jesus taught that if we do not forgive others, He will not forgive us. "Why?" you ask. Could it be that our Lord knows it is impossible for us to effectively minister Christ's compassionate nature to others, when we ourselves are polluted with resentment, bitterness, anger, hurt, unforgiveness, wounded pride, and arrogance? We must allow God to touch *our* lives, helping us to let go of the pollutant of unforgiveness—*then* God can flow through a clear channel to touch the lives of others (cf. Jam. 3:8-4:12). Forgiveness is also a key to our physical and spiritual health.

Peter dealt with this "forgiving problem," too. *"Peter came to [Jesus] and said, 'Lord, how often shall my brother sin against me, and I forgive him? Up to seven times?' Jesus said to him, 'I do not say to you up to seven times, but up to seventy times seven' [or times without number]"* (Mat. 18:21-22 NKJV). In other words, don't keep tally of

100

offenses—just keep forgiving! On the other hand, God is not requiring us to "enable" habitual offenders to continue in unchecked destructive ways. There is a time for intervention and a time to offer constructive teaching and suggestions.

Some of our problems are caused by our own wrong doing. It is not enough for Jesus to simply forgive us—we need to do our part. To the man who was healed at the pool of Bethesda, Jesus said, *"Behold, thou art made whole: sin no more, lest a worse thing come unto thee"* (Jn. 5:14).

Our Savior's compassion not only prompts Him to alleviate our pain, guilt, and the results of our disordered lives—He goes a step further. He teaches that we must *turn* from "wrong living" to "right living"—from *death* to *life!* For instance, a responsible parent will not only forgive an erring child—but, will also lovingly *correct* or *punish* the child so that the right path of life will be followed. Yet, even in this parental role, forgiving (i.e., cancelling of offenses) is imperative if the child is going to be able to *grow* through experiences and mistakes (cf. Eph. 6:4). The cancelling of past offenses lifts the weights of the past, so one can excel in the future!

True FORGIVING is to excuse for a fault or offence; to renounce resentment in regard to past offenses; and to absolve from payment for offenses. To be human is to keep tally of offenses—to be Christlike is to totally forgive those who have offended us! Only God can bring that kind of forgiveness into our lives! And, only that kind of forgiveness will free the offended to extend Christ's compassionate nature. Sometimes that may involve confrontation of the offence and sometimes it may involve silently overlooking an offence.

Once we truly understand the meaning of forgiveness we are able to translate Jesus' compassionate nature into action!

LOVE is basic to godliness! It is impossible to be a godly person and at the same time portray a harsh judgmental attitude toward those who have made mistakes or are lost in sin. "GOD *IS* LOVE" (I Jn. 4:8). Love at its highest level describes the very essence of God. True love is such a powerful reality that it even covers a multitude of sins! (I Pet. 4:8). Real love has pure motives and keeps no record of wrongs (I Cor. 13:4-7).

When Jesus was asked, "What is the great commandment in the law?"—He responded, *"Thou shalt love the Lord thy God with all thy heart, and with all thy soul, and with all thy mind [Dt. 6:5]. This is the first and great commandment. And the second is like unto it, Thou shalt love thy neighbor as thyself [Lev. 19:18]. On these two commandments hang all the law and the prophets"* (Mt. 22:36-40).

But Jesus' message of love went further than this. His message was revolutionary, for he taught that our love should extend even to our *enemies!* (Mt. 5:43-47). And, not only did he teach this, he actually died for his enemies! *"While we were yet sinners, Christ died for us....When we were ENEMIES, we were reconciled to God by the death of his Son"* (Rom. 5:8-10).

Having heard the love message from Jesus, the subject is very prominent in John's writings:

"Dear friends, let us love one another, for love comes from God. Everyone who loves has been born of God and knows God. Whoever does not love does not know God, because God is love...If we love one another, God lives in us and his love is made complete in us....Whoever lives in love lives in God, and God in him....If anyone says, 'I love God,' yet hates his brother, he is a liar. For if anyone who does not love his brother, whom he has seen, cannot love God, whom he has not seen. And he has given us this command: Whoever loves God must also love his brother" (I Jn. 4:7-21 NIV).

102

Genuine Christianity requires the Christian to love the fatherless and destitute—to be *doers* of the Word and not hearers only! (Jam. 1:22-27). James wrote that by our showing partiality to the rich who oppress the poor, we actually join with those who "blaspheme that worthy name" by which we are called, by failing to love others without partiality and oppression. He said, *"If ye fulfil the royal law according to the scripture, Thou shalt love thy neighbor as thyself, ye do well: But if ye have respect to persons, ye commit sin, and are convinced of the law as transgressors"* (cf. Jam. 2:1-9, esp. vs. 8-9). This type of love is not just condescending kind *words* or *thoughts* toward the needy, but rather requires *"love in action."*

True love will cause us to get involved, to invest our energies and resources, to feel the hurt and pain of the oppressed enough to help them—enough to make a *difference* in their lives!

LOVE is defined as an intense affectionate concern for another person and their welfare; unconditional benevolent concern for the well-being of another which surpasses one's own desire for comfort, safety, or satisfaction of personal comfort and needs.

ACCEPTANCE of every kind of person was pivotal to the success of Jesus' ministry. The world (and the *carnal* church!) *rejects* those who are different or inferior. Jesus beckoned people to come to Him *with* their sin, defilement, confusion, sickness, and bondage. They did not have to change first! Association with *Him* automatically brought the changes which caused His followers to measure-up to an acceptable standard. Consider the woman caught in the act of adultery, the immoral woman who washed Jesus' feet with her tears, Zacchaeus the tax collector, and the rough-hewn fishermen He called to be His disciples, to name a few!

The parable of the prodigal son demonstrates Jesus' acceptance of those in the mire of sin (Lk. 15:11-24). Acceptance of one needing to change, *precedes* the changing. The father came to meet the prodigal with a robe and ring—and announced he was throwing a party to celebrate his son's return *before* the son took a bath—*before* he was rehabilitated—*before* he was detoxified—*before* he apologized for his waywardness! We say, "Lord, you change them and I'll love them." He whispers, **"You love them and I will change them"** (see Mt. 5:43-48). We must not confuse "acceptance," of course, with condoning sinful life-styles. We accept the sinner, not the sin—and wait patiently as God does the convicting, changing, and renewing.

This character quality called *acceptance* also breaks down the walls of prejudice based on national or ethnic background. It reaches out to those who are incarcerated, those who have become old and feeble, and those who are physically, mentally or emotionally handicapped. Too often, these people are shunned or ignored. If Jesus' character is within us, we will be challenged to find ways to communicate Christ's acceptance of these hurting people who are often made to feel that they have no worth!

Years ago I knew a family that was asked not to bring their retarded son to their fashionable church any longer—he was considered a distraction. Wounded and confused, they finally found a congregation that gladly accepted the boy—along with his two lovely sisters. People who make up a compassionate congregation will not only *accept* those who are *different* or who have *special needs*, they will be *creative* in finding wisdom and resources to meet the needs of *all* their people. The result?—they have special ministry opportunities for the physically challenged, the mentally challenged, the hearing impaired, the blind, those with learning disabilities, etc.

Crystal Cathedral of southern California began their worship services in a drive-in theater. Their vision included reaching out to those who found it difficult to attend Church due to disabilities. I know of Churches which have special services for the deaf or who provide a person to "sign" for the deaf in the regular services. I have heard of Christian education programs which include classes for special children who would find the curriculum of a regular class too difficult.

Accept people as they are. *Then* introduce them to our compassionate Lord—the sin and defects will drop off as they get to know Him. *Reject* people because of their sin, abnormalities or dissimilarities—and the *sin, abnormalities,* or *dissimilarities* are *reinforced,* causing *further* barriers. It is impossible to extend either forgiveness or love, unless we are willing to accept people right where they are—*before* they apologize—*before* they put their lives in order—*before* they are lovely!

ACCEPTANCE is defined as the act of willingly or gladly accepting another as satisfactory or acceptable regardless of status, condition, or qualification.

MERCY was a part of Jesus' daily life. Jesus could *accept* people just as they were, because *mercy* was *basic* to his character and mode of operation (Lk. 7:36-50). His mercy *compelled* him to leave those who had not strayed in order to *seek the lost one,* as He exemplified in the parable of the lost sheep (Lk. 15:3-7). He showed mercy to the woman caught in adultery (Jn. 8:3-11). The merciless accusers were also guilty of sinning, and would have stoned her! That's hypocrisy! We see Jesus showing mercy throughout the Gospels, even as He has shown mercy to us (I Pet. 1:3).

God's mercy extends to all who need it! (Heb. 8:12). We are able to experience new life because of His mercy toward us! (Eph. 2:1-7; Heb. 2:14-18). Mercy has to do with pardon and clemency (i.e. to mercifully moderate the severity of punishment). The *wages* of sin is *death,* but because of God's mercy He has shown *clemency* to us—pardoning us from the death sentence—giving us FREEDOM and ABUNDANT LIFE (cf. Jn. 8:36; 10:10). That is God's mercy in action!

We, too, are *commanded* to be merciful. Jesus said *"Be merciful, just as your Father is merciful. Do not judge, and you will not be judged. Do not condemn, and you will not be condemned. Forgive, and you will be forgiven"* (Luke 6:36-37 NIV). Solomon said, *"The merciful man does good for his own soul, but he who is cruel troubles his own flesh"* (Prov. 11:17 NKJV).

And more wisdom for living: *"He who despises his neighbor sins; but he who has mercy on the poor, happy is he. Do they not go astray who devise evil? But mercy and truth belong to those who devise good....He who oppresses the poor reproaches his Maker, but he who honors Him has mercy on the needy"* (Prov. 14:21-22, 31 NKJV). Again, the manifesto of the Kingdom of God called for people to show mercy, instead of judgment. According to Jesus, if we fail to show mercy, it will be to our own hurt: *"Blessed are the merciful: for they shall obtain mercy"* (Mt. 5:7).

Jesus was merciful to *all* sinners. But, it seems that some Christians today are more concerned with being anti-gay, anti-abortion, anti-sin. Perhaps we should reconsider our mode of operation. These people are loved by God and they need to know we love them, even though we do not love what they do. We are *all* sinners who need a Savior. If God could change *us*, can He not change *others* without our condemning them? If they come to know the Lord—their ways will change!

Somehow there are some who feel they are "compromising" their standards if they show mercy to those who have been responsible for heinous sins which have hurt the cause of Christ. But this isn't so. Once again, look at the *mercy* God extended to Paul! He was among the worst persecutors of Christians. He testified with great conviction, *"Christ Jesus came into the world to save sinners, of whom I am chief. However, for this reason I obtained mercy, that in me first Jesus Christ might show all longsuffering, as a pattern to those who are going to believe on Him for everlasting life"* (I Tim. 1:15-16). Through God's *mercy,* Paul became even more zealous as a Christian than he was as an enemy of Christ. The *extending* of *mercy* to those in our day who are crusading against Christian values, has the potential of bringing forth modern-day Pauls and Paulines!

This is illustrated by the changed life of the woman whose court challenge brought about the "Roe vs. Wade" Supreme Court ruling. Before nation-wide TV, she told how a lady from "the other side" reached out to her in love—accepting her right where she was. While others marched, waving their posters and yelling out inflaming statements that only made the people angry, this Christian lady found a way into a heart after the manner of her Savior! In time this Christian who understood the "dynamic of acceptance" took Ms. Roe to Church where she felt the power of God, resulting in her finding Jesus as her own personal Savior! Now she's a "new creation"— with *new* values!

We'll never win the world by rejecting people for what they do or don't do—or for what they do or do not believe! *Love* covers a multitude of sins, enabling the Christian to *accept* the errant ones right where they are—showing *mercy* rather than condemnation.

MERCY can be defined as the compassionate treatment of an offender or enemy; a disposition to be kind and forgiving. If God's character dwells within us, we will be full of mercy! (cf. Jam. 3:17; Lk. 6:36).

E VANGELISM was the natural outgrowth of Jesus' compassionate life and ministry. Jesus, the Light of the world (Jn. 8:12), spread the Good News of the Kingdom of Light through both his message and his actions. He freed people from the bondage and darkness of the "law without love" (cf. Jn. 12:35-36, 46). His new commandment of Love was revolutionary—setting up a new precedent by which we also are instructed to live and minister. Even as people were drawn to His message when He was on earth, this message still draws people today.

The source of light is *fire*—whether it comes from huge explosions of the sun, a campfire, lantern, or electric light bulb. Fire brings warmth and illumination—and it attracts people to come closer—to bask in its warmth and light. There is a light that shines forth from the face of every Christian which is ignited in the inner man by the fire of the Holy Spirit. People are attracted to that light—even though they may seem to reject the light. We must not hide that light or allow the light in our lives to grow dim.

I remember a gathering of thousands of people in a large stadium where everyone was given a small candle. I witnessed the overwhelming brightening of the stadium as the crowd passed light from one to another—until bright glowing light *overcame* the darkness. What a sight!—and what an *insight* to the difference that *one* can make when cooperating with others.

Jewish religious leaders put heavy burdens upon people, yet were often bound by the very sins of which they accused others. But Jesus was different! He was *pure* and *compassionate*. He *forgave* instead of judging. He *loved* instead of hating. He *accepted* people right where they were instead of rejecting them. He was *merciful* instead of pitiless and vindictive. He spread the Good News of liberation from bondage and hurt! (Isa. 61:1-4).

Many people already *know* they are sinners. They know they fall short. The world is suffering from an epidemic of rejection and inferiority complexes. No wonder

108

they respond to Forgiveness, Love, Acceptance and Mercy—resulting in Evangelism of the lost multitudes. This should ignite a burning desire inside of each of us to spread the Good News that will set people free! (Matt. 4:23-25).

Jesus commanded *us* to let *our light* so shine, that others will want to glorify God when they see the good works that emanate from those who are His followers (Mt. 5:14-16). *"Arise shine...darkness shall cover the earth, and gross darkness the people; but the Lord shall arise upon thee, and his glory shall arise upon thee...and the Gentiles shall come to thy light..."* (Isa. 60:1-3).

F.L.A.M.E.—a life-giving, cleansing fire from God! But alas, **leave out a FORGIVING HEART**, and we will be seriously crippled in our efforts to walk in Love, Acceptance, Mercy, and Evangelism: **FLAME without the "F" (forgiveness) is LAME!** A spiritually lame (crippled) individual or Church will just limp along— always falling short of God's best! No wonder some Churches never excel in evangelism—i.e., reaching out to the lost and bringing them to Christ.

Perhaps we, as Christians, should do some soul searching! Unforgiveness in the heart is actually the outgrowth of a combination of serious "heart diseases." James wrote:

> *"Who is wise and understanding among you? Let him show by good conduct that his works are done in the meekness of wisdom. But if you have bitter envy and self-seeking in your hearts, do not boast and lie against the truth. This wisdom does not descend from above, but is earthly, sensual, demonic. For where envy and self-seeking exist, confusion and every evil thing will be there. But the wisdom that is from above is first pure, then peaceable, gentle, willing to yield, full of mercy and good fruits, without partiality and without hypocrisy. Now the fruit of righteousness is sown in peace by those who make peace"* (Jam. 3:13-18 NKJV).

After we go to the Great Physician for some "open heart surgery," we will have the pure heart that is required for effective evangelism—full of an attitude of compassion, care, concern and commitment.

EVANGELISM is defined as the zealous, enthusiastic preaching and dissemination of the Gospel (good news) of Jesus Christ. His actions spoke louder than His words. The people saw His message in action and multitudes flocked to Him.

Let's fan the flame! The F.L.A.M.E. that burst forth from the life of Jesus has never been totally extinguished. False teaching, oppression, persecution, hypocrisy, legalism, and tribulation, like cold water, have been doused onto the fire of Christianity over the centuries. Sometimes the fire has smoldered into little more than smoke and nearly died out—only to burst out again. The beauty and attraction of the brilliant fire is even more spectacular when compared to the dark and smoky seasons. No demon, institution, law, false religion, or philosophy can stop the combustion of Christ's compassionate nature and life (cf. Rom. 8:31-39).

Let us allow God to *torch us* with His F.L.A.M.E! When we are ablaze with the firelight that first emanates from Him—then we, too, will be able to shed light to those around us who are wandering in the darkness. *"You are the light of the world...let your light shine before men, that they may see your good deeds and praise your Father in heaven"* (Mt. 5:14-16).

Chapter 11

"Sir, We Would See Jesus"

(John 12:21)

—by Ralph Woodrow

The great theme of the Bible is Jesus Christ. The Old Testament types and shadows point to him. In the New Testament he is revealed as the Lord from heaven. The *first* verse of the New Testament (Matt. 1:1) begins by talking about Jesus Christ; the *last* verse (Rev. 22:21) ends by mentioning Him. He is mentioned at the beginning and the end; he is "alpha and omega, the beginning and the end" (Rev. 1:8).

It has now been nearly two thousand years since the very one who made this world became a man and lived among men. "He was in the world, and the world was made by him, and the world knew him not" (John 1:3,10). He is the artistic designer and architect who took the hammer of omnipotence, hit it upon the anvil of time, and sent sparks into the heavens producing brilliant stars, many of which are thousands of times larger than this earth. He took the paint brush of diety and painted the sky blue and it has been blue ever since! He upholdeth all things by the word of his power (Heb. 1:2,3).

How strange and wonderful that this princely youth from the little town of Nazareth should be the chief engineer of all things! Can a man look at huge mountains, the oceans, and the worlds out there in space without feeling a strong reverence toward the author of these mammoth works? How amazing that he who was *infinite* became an *infant,* so small a woman carried him in her arms.

He left heaven where rivers never freeze, winds never blow, frosts never chill, flowers never fade, where there is no sickness or death. He left the ivory palaces above and put on *humanity* that we might put on *divinity.* He became the son of *man* that we might become the sons of *God.* "As many as received him, to them gave he power to become the sons of God" (John 1:12).

He grew up in obscurity. He had no wealth. He attended no college. Yet the record says: "Never man spake like this man" (John 7:46). His relatives were inconspicuous folk living in a rural community. Yet in infancy he frightened a king; in boyhood he puzzled the doctors of the law, possessing greater wisdom than all of them put together; in manhood he ruled the elements. He defied the law of gravitation by walking on the water. He spoke peace to a raging sea and it carried him as gently as a mother would take her child.

He healed multitudes without medicine and made no charge for his services. He fed a hungry multitude with the lunch of a small boy. He broke up funerals. He gave life back to those who were dead, announcing the glad news: "I am the resurrection, and the life" (John 11:25). Though he was the Lord from heaven, he sat in the kitchens of small homes and ate with poor people. He tilted back his chair, visited with the people he had created, and sometimes even spent the night. The next morning, he who made the whole round world would say goodbye, and walk down the dusty road.

When he was born, there was no room for him in the inn. But since that time, *millions* have made room for him in their hearts. His presence has brought peace and joy. "Christ in you the hope of glory" (Col. 1:27). He was born *contrary* to the laws of birth. He lived *contrary* to the laws of life. He died *contrary* to the laws of death. He arose *contrary* to the grave. He ascended into heaven *contrary* to the laws of gravitation. He will some day return *contrary* to the desires of wicked men!

He laid aside his royal robe for the gown of a peasant. He was rich but for our sakes he became poor (2 Cor. 8:9). He didn't own the straw on which he was born. He didn't own the boat in which he sailed. He didn't own the beast on which he rode. He didn't own the grave in which he was buried. He was born in another man's stable; he sailed in another man's boat; he rode on another man's beast; he was buried in another man's tomb. One time he said, "The foxes have holes, and the birds of the air have nests, but the Son of Man has nowhere to lay his head" (Matt. 8:20). He was poor, yet he owned everything!

He never wrote a song, yet he has furnished the theme for more songs than all song writers combined. He never founded a college and yet all the schools in the world cannot boast the number of students who have studied under him! He never mobilized an army or drafted a soldier, yet no military leader has ever enlisted as many volunteers as those who serve him.

Centuries before he came into this world, Isaiah prophesied: "For unto us a child is born, unto us a son is given: and the government shall be upon his shoulder: and his name shall be called Wonderful, Counseller, The mighty God, The everlasting Father, The Prince of Peace" (Isa. 9:6).

You do not need to be an *astronomer* to understand he is the Sun of Righteousness with healing in his wings. You do not need to be a *geologist* to understand he is the Rock of Ages and the Rock that is higher than I. You do not need to be a *zoologist* to understand he is the Lamb of God and the Lion of the tribe of Judah. You do not need to be a *botanist* to understand that he is the Rose of Sharon and the Lily of the Valley. You do not need to be a *musician* to understand he is the Great Harmonizer of all discords. You do not need to be a *doctor* to understand he is the Healer of all human ills.

Great men have come and gone. Jesus lives on! Herod could not kill him. People at a religious service could not stone him. Satan could not tempt him. Death could not destroy him. The grave could not contain him. The story of Jesus Christ is the greatest story ever told.

Jesus is the only man to ever live on earth in whom moral perfection found complete expression with no mixture of good and evil. He was not as other men of history whose virtues have caused them to be praised and whose vices have caused them to be condemned. There was no combination of good and evil in him. He was not merely a son of God; he was THE son of God.

Have you ever heard someone make a statement like: "Jesus was a good man and a great teacher, but no more than this"? This statement is self-contradictory. If Jesus was a good man and a great teacher, then we should accept what he taught about himself—that he was the Son of God. If he was not who he claimed to be, he was either a liar or a lunatic. If he was a liar or a lunatic, he was not a good man *or* a great teacher!

The study of doctrine, or prophecy, or religious history certainly has its place. But unless these things are Christ-centered, they miss the mark. Even Paul, with his education and vast knowledge of truth, realized the message must be "Jesus Christ and him crucified" (1 Cor. 2:2), lest people be robbed of the "simplicity that is in Christ" (2 Cor. 11:3).

Profound sermons about the "Symbolic Significance Of The Knotholes On Noah's Ark" or "How Many Warts Will The Antichrist Have On His Left Toe?" can never match or replace the old, old story of Jesus and his love! Any sermon, regardless of subject, falls short of its best objectives if it fails to properly exalt him who is our great example, Jesus Christ!

It is a sad state of things when people seek success without the Savior, healing without the Healer, gifts without the Giver, victory without the Victor, revelation without the Revelator, or Christianity without Christ.

Jesus was not a philosopher searching for truth. He was truth! He was not a mystic. He was reality. He was not a reformer. He was a transformer. He was not a visionary. He was the light of the world. He never reasoned; he knew. He knew why he came; from where he came; and where he was going. He knew who he was; he knew what he could do, and what the devil *could not do!*

Jesus Christ is not one of the great religious leaders of the *past,* he is in the *now.* He is the great I AM. He said: "I am the bread, I am the light, I am the door, I am the good shepherd, I am the son of God, I am the resurrection, I am the life, I am the way, I am the truth, I am the vine, I am the alpha and omega, I am the Lord I change not." He is "the same yesterday, and today, and forever"—a changeless Christ in a changing world (Heb. 13:8). "He is before all things, and by him all things consist" (Col. 1:15-19).

Followers of the world's religions can take us to the tombs of their founders. Or we can visit the tombs of famous presidents like Abraham Lincoln at Springfield, Illinois, or the tomb of George Washington at Mount Vernon. The British have their Westminster Abbey where they bury their noble dead. We have visited the tombs of Abraham and Sarah in Hebron. But as Christians we rejoice, not in some beautifully decorated tomb under oriental skies, for Jesus rose again and is alive forevermore! We stand with joy before the open door of an *empty tomb.*

We are not worshiping a helpless infant lying in a manger of straw. We are not worshiping a little boy standing in the temple answering the questions of the doctors of the law. We are not worshiping a teacher standing by the shores of Galilee. We are not worshiping a dead body hanging limp on a cross. We are not worshiping a wrapped mummy. We are worshiping the one who

115

is NOW "King of kings and Lord of lords" (1 Tim. 6:15). It is not a case of him being crowned king at some future day, he has already ascended into heaven and been crowned Lord of all (Acts 2:36).

Jesus is holy, pure, immaculate, and it would be impossible for him to sin. Since he himself is the very essense of truth, it would be impossible for him to lie. He owns all things visible and invisible, so it is impossible for him to steal. He is the author of wisdom and justice so it is impossible for him to misjudge. He is infallible; therefore it would be impossible for him to make a mistake. He was, is, and always will be altogether lovely, perfect, sinless, and pure.

In spite of this, we read that "he came unto his own and his own received him not," he was "despised and rejected of men" (John 1:12; Isa. 53:3). Consider the false accusations that were made against him:

CRAZY, INSANE: "He is mad" (John 10:20).

DOUBT CAUSER, NEGATIVE. "How long wilt thou make us doubt?" (John 10:24).

BLASPHEMER: "We stone thee for blasphemy" (John 10:33).

BASTARD: "Where is thy father?" (John 8:19).

KEEPER OF BAD COMPANY: "Why eateth your master with publicans and sinners?" (Matthew 9:11).

UNGODLY: "This man is not of God" (John 9:16).

SINNER: "We know this man is a sinner" (John 10:33).

DECEIVER: "He deceiveth the people" (John 7:12).

DIVIDER, DIVISION-MAKER: "...a division among the people because of him" (John 7:43).

DEMON POSSESSED: "Thou hast a devil" (John 7:20).

A PERSECUTION COMPLEX: "Who goeth about to kill thee?" (John 7:20).

PROVOKER TO ANGER: "Are you angry with me, because I have made a man every whit whole?" (John 7:23).

UNRECOMMENDED BY RELIGIOUS LEADERS: "Have any of the rulers of the Pharisees believed on him?" (John 7:48).

116

LIAR: "Thou barest record of thyself, thy record is not true" (John 8:13).

SUICIDAL: "Will he kill himself?" (John 8:22).

BOASTER: "Whom maketh thyself?" (John 8:53).

BEELZEBUB: "They have called the master...Beelzebub" (Matt. 10:25).

UNEDUCATED: "How knoweth this man letters, having never learned?" (John 7:15).

LOW CLASS: "Can any good thing come out of Nazareth?" (John 1:46).

FALSE PROPHET: "Out of Galilee ariseth no prophet" (John 7:52).

HALFBREED: "Thou art a Samaritan" (John 8:48).

DISHONORABLE: "Ye do dishonor me" (John 8:49).

LABORER: "Is this not the carpenter?" (Mk. 6:3).

Finally certain ones cried out for his death. He was rejected as a traitor to his country, a heretic by his church, an outcast from his family. See Him as he prays in the garden. See Him as his own disciples turn against Him. See Him as he is cruelly driven through an illegal trial. See Him as he leaves Pilate's hall. See the stained gown badly torn, hanging from his shoulders. His bare feet are leaving spots of blood on the cobblestone pavement. His back is bleeding from the stripes inflicted thereon. His face is covered with spittle. His hair is tangled in dry clots of blood produced by the beatings. A crown of thorns is pushed down upon his head.

At Golgotha wicked men nail his hands to an old rugged cross—piercing his hands that had done only good. Hands that laid the foundations of the earth and stretched out the heavens like a scroll—hands that scooped out the valleys and piled up the mountains—hands that unrolled a carpet of grass for humans to walk upon and laced the earth with babbling brooks and flowing streams—hands that placed a furnace in the sun and started our solar system turning! (Heb. 1:10). His hands had blessed little children, had healed the sick, had opened

117

the eyes of the blind, had demonstrated the blessing of the kingdom of heaven on earth. Now the men he made and came to redeem were nailing his hands to the cross.

Earlier Jesus had predicted exactly how he would die—that it would be by crucifixion. "And I, if I be lifted up from the earth, will draw all men unto me. This he said, *signifying what death he should die"* (John 12:32,33). This is remarkable, for in predicting his death, Jesus made it clear he would not die by old age. His death would not come because of sickness. His death would not come from being drowned on the sea of Galilee. His death would not come by being stoned, as was the Jewish custom, but by being *lifted up,* the Roman form of capital punishment.

"Greater love hath no man than this, that a man lay down his life for his friends" (John 15:13). There have been men who have laid down their lives for those they loved—for their friends. Human love can go no further than this. But the love of Christ is greater than this: not only did he lay down his life for his FRIENDS, he died for his ENEMIES! "For scarcely for a righteous man will one die; yet peradverture for a good man some would even dare to die. *But* God commendeth his love toward us, in that, while we were yet *sinners,* Christ died for us...when we were *enemies,* we were reconciled to God by the death of his Son" (Rom. 5:7,8).

"Surely he hath borne OUR griefs, and carried OUR sorrows: yet we did esteem him stricken, smitten of God, and afflicted. But he was wounded for OUR transgressions, he was bruised for OUR iniquities: the chastisement of OUR peace was upon him; and with his stripes WE are healed" (Isa. 53:4,5). It was not for his own sins he died—he had none. It was for our griefs, our sorrows, our transgressions, our iniquities, our peace, and by his stripes we are healed.

The three crosses—on which two thieves and the son of God were hanging together at Calvary—stood in crisp, black silhouette against the darkened light of the sky. The earth beneath the feet of weeping men and women began to tremble from some vast, inner convulsion. Messengers, fleeing from the temple courts panted the frightening news that the veil of the holy of holies had been torn from top to bottom by invisible hands, a sign of dreadful and mysterious portent.

Those who think of Jesus only as a "good man" or a "great teacher" may follow him to the tomb, and there, they suppose, it all ended. But if this were the case, if there was no resurrection, *what became of the body?*

One theory that surfaced at an early point was that the *disciples* stole the body of Jesus and hid it. Jewish leaders, fearing how far the message of the resurrection might advance, actually paid money to the soldiers who guarded the tomb to promote this lie! They "gave large money unto the soldiers, saying, Say ye, His disciples came by night, and stole him away while we slept. And if this come to the governor's ears, we will persuade him and secure you. So they took the money, and did as they were taught: and this saying is commonly reported among the Jews until this day" (Matt. 28:12-15).

Of course this theory is silly right on the surface. If the body was stolen away while the guards were *asleep,* how would they know *who* did it?

It could not have been the disciples that took the body, for in the discouragement of those events that led to Jesus' death and burial, the disciples themselves did not believe he would be resurrected. They did *not* understand the scripture "that he must rise again from the dead" (John 20:9). Even when Mary Magdalene saw the empty tomb, she supposed someone had taken the body away (verse 13). When she and those women with her actually saw the risen Christ, they ran to tell the disciples, but "their words seemed to them as *idle tales,* and they believed them *not*" (Lk. 24:10,11). Obviously these

119

men had not taken the body away. They were not trying to fabricate a resurrection hoax.

Only after Jesus himself appeared to them and showed himself alive by "many infallible proofs" (Acts 1:3) were they convinced. Thomas, who ultimately investigated his wounds and believed, was not the only doubter.

If the disciples had taken the body, they would have returned to their worldly pursuits and most assuredly not put their own lives on the line by preaching the resurrection. But being totally convinced of the reality of the resurrection, they were willing to face the impending persecution. In time Christians were thrown to wild beasts, were stoned, were sawn asunder, were hung upside down, were burned at the stake. It was not the disciples that took the body of Jesus—*men do not become martyrs for something they know is untrue!*

It was not the disciples—the friends of Jesus—that took the body. Could it have been his *enemies?* This will not fit either. As the disciples began to tell of the resurrection of Christ, thousands believed the message. Jewish leaders who had cried out for Jesus' death were greatly perplexed. If they had taken the body of Jesus, they could have produced it, disproved the resurrection message, and Christianity would have come to a screeching halt. Obviously they did not have the body! If they had the body, it would not have been necessary for them to pay the guards to lie.

If the disciples did not take the body, if the enemies of Christ did not take the body, then what happened? As Christians, we believe the tomb was empty because of the RESURRECTION! It is at the very heart of the gospel. Were it not for the resurrection, there would be no Christianity. Even if Jesus had lived a sinless life, had overcome every temptation, had shed his blood and died—even with all of this, we would have no salvation—were it not for the *resurrection.* A dead savior could never give life.

As Paul phrased it: "If Christ be not risen, then is our preaching vain, and your faith is also vain" (1 Cor. 15:14). But because he lives, we shall live also.

A familiar hymn says:

> *He lives! He lives! Christ Jesus lives today.*
> *He walks with me and talks with me,*
> *Along life's narrow way.*
> *He lives! He lives! salvation to impart.*
> *You ask me how I know he lives,*
> *He lives within my heart.*

Recognizing Jesus Christ as the great theme of the Bible, some have described Him from each biblical book in the following manner:

In Genesis he is the SEED OF THE WOMAN.

In Exodus he is the PASSOVER LAMB.

In Leviticus he is our HIGH PRIEST.

In Numbers he is the FIERY PILLAR.

In Deuteronomy he is the PROPHET LIKE UNTO MOSES.

In Joshua he is the CAPTAIN OF OUR SALVATION.

In Judges he is our RIGHTEOUS JUDGE.

In Ruth he is our KINSMAN-REDEEMER.

In First and Second Samuel he is our TRUSTED PROPHET.

In Kings and Chronicles he is our REIGNING KING.

In Ezra he is our FAITHFUL SCRIBE.

In Nehemiah he is the REBUILDER OF BROKEN WALLS.

In Esther he is our MORDECAI.

In Job he is our EVER-LIVING REDEEMER.

In Psalms he is our SHEPHERD.

In Proverbs and Ecclesiastes he is our WISDOM.

In the Song of Solomon he is our BRIDEGROOM.

In Isaiah he is the PRINCE OF PEACE.

In Jeremiah he is the RIGHTEOUS BRANCH.

In Lamentations he is our WEEPING PROPHET.

In Ezekiel he is the PLANT OF RENOWN.

In Daniel he is the FOURTH MAN.

Who is Jesus Christ?

In Hosea he is the FAITHFUL HUSBAND.
In Joel he is the BAPTIZER WITH THE HOLY SPIRIT.
In Amos he is our BURDEN BEARER.
In Obadiah he is the MIGHTY TO SAVE.
In Jonah he is our MISSIONARY.
In Micah he is the MESSENGER OF BEAUTIFUL FEET.
In Nahum he is the AVENGER OF GOD'S ELECT.
In Habakkuk he is GOD'S EVANGELIST.
In Zephaniah he is our SAVIOR.
In Haggai he is the RESTORER OF GOD'S HERITAGE.
In Zachariah he is the FOUNTAIN FOR SIN.
In Malachi he is the SUN OF RIGHTEOUSNESS.

Who is Jesus Christ?

In Matthew he is the MESSIAH.
In Mark he is the WONDER-WORKER.
In Luke he is the SON OF MAN.
In John he is the SON OF GOD.
In Acts he is our PENTECOST.
In Romans he is our JUSTIFIER.
In Corinthians he is our SANCTIFIER.
In Galatians he is our REDEEMER FROM THE CURSE.
In Ephesians he is UNSEARCHABLE RICHES.
In Philippians he is our NEED SUPPLIER.
In Colossians he is the FULNESS OF THE GODHEAD.
In Thessalonians he is our COMING KING.
In Timothy the MEDIATOR BETWEEN GOD AND MAN.
In Titus he is our FAITHFUL PASTOR.
In Philemon he is a FRIEND CLOSER THAN A BROTHER.
In Hebrews he is the BLOOD OF THE COVENANT.
In James he is our GREAT PHYSICIAN.
In First and Second Peter he is our CHIEF SHEPHERD.
In First, Second, and Third John he is LOVE.
In Jude he is the LORD WITH TEN THOUSANDS
   OF HIS SAINTS.
In Revelation he is KING OF KINGS AND LORD OF
   LORDS.

Chapter 12

GOING HOME ANOTHER WAY

—by Ralph Woodrow

They had traveled far, these wise men from the east. Upon their arrival at Jerusalem, they asked around: "Where is he that is born King of the Jews? for we have seen his star in the east, and are come to worship him."

Soon the entire city of Jerusalem was "troubled" by this inquiry, including Herod. When he demanded of the Jewish religious leaders where the Messiah would be born, they pointed him to Micah's prophecy —that "in Bethlehem" would he be born, "a Governor, that shall rule my people Israel." Strangely, Herod took this prophecy seriously—so seriously, in fact, that he considered this new king a threat to his kingdom!

Pretending that he wanted to worship this one who was destined to be the "King of the Jews," he commissioned the wise men to go to Bethlehem, find the baby, and let him know. Apparently they did not realize he had murder in his heart, and would have returned to him with the information. But,

"...being warned of God in a dream that they should not return to Herod, THEY DEPARTED INTO THEIR OWN COUNTRY ANOTHER WAY" (Matt. 2:1-12).

Some translators use terms such as stargazers (Williams) and astrologers (Goodspeed)—to describe these men from the east. Others call them magicians (Moffatt) or Magi (Weymouth). The similarity between the terms magicians and magi is apparent. Others, as in the King James Version, simply call them wise men. Opinions may vary as to why they are called *wise* men, but one good reason for calling them wise would be that *they were seeking Jesus!* Today, wise men still seek him!

Many are familiar with the lovely old hymn: "We three kings of Orient are; bearing gifts we traverse afar, field and fountain, moor and mountain, following yonder star." But the Bible does not actually call them *kings,* nor does it say there were *three* of them! The number three might be assumed from the three gifts offered—gold, frankincense, and myrrh—and, right or wrong, a tradition has assigned to them the names Balthasar, Gaspar, and Melcheir.

Following the birth of Jesus, in that horrid massacre known as The Slaughter of the Innocents, Herod ordered the death of all males two years old and under in Bethlehem and its vicinity (Matt. 2:16). A note in the NIV Bible says: "The number has often been exaggerated as being in the thousands. In so small a village as Bethlehem, however (even with the surrounding area included), the number was probably not large."

Even if we estimate the population of this area as high as 2,000 people—figuring ages from those just born up to age 80—this would average out to 50 babies under two years of age. But since only males were involved, this would cut the number in half. Of this number, it is possible that some escaped, as the baby Jesus did, when Joseph and Mary fled into Egypt. *The Pulpit Commentary* estimates it was not over 20. Obviously, we don't know the exact number killed in this brutal slaughter, but it was not thousands.

In their journey from the east to Jerusalem, the wise men had probably traveled a thousand miles, a trip which would have taken weeks to accomplish. The final leg of the journey from Jerusalem to Bethlehem was short—only five miles. Many have not realized this closeness. I suppose I knew it vaguely, but the impact of it came with my first trip to the area, in 1978, when the drive from Jerusalem to Bethlehem only took a few minutes.

Herod told the wise men to go to Bethlehem and find the baby and return to him with the information. The title Herod means "Hero," but he was no hero. He had a horrible reputation. At a later time, Jesus called one of the Herods a "fox" (Lk. 13:32). Whether the wise men actually promised to return to him or not, we are not told. To be safe, they could have said: "...the Lord willing."

To include the phrase, "the Lord willing," is certainly scriptural. In the book of James we read: "Go to now, you that say, Today or tomorrow we will go into such a city, and continue there a year, and buy and sell, and get gain: whereas you know not what shall be on the morrow....For what you ought to say, *If the Lord will,* we shall live, and do this, or that" (James 4:13-15).

On his way into town, a man boasted to his neighbor about what he was going to buy and do in town. The neighbor, being a Christian, told him he ought to say, "The Lord willing." The man scoffed at this, explaining that he had the money and was going to do just what he said! But before he got to town, some thugs beat him up, took all his money, and left him bruised and bleeding. Finally he started back home. When the neighbor saw him as he passed by, he asked where he was going. "I'm going home," he answered, and was careful to add: "THE LORD WILLING!"

It was not God's will that the wise men return to Herod. Instead, being warned of God in a dream, they WENT HOME ANOTHER WAY. From these words we have gleaned the title for this message and to which we will make a spiritual application: God changes lives.

There is the case of Legion of Gadera, for example (Mk. 5:1-20). After Jesus had calmed a storm on the sea of Galilee, arriving at the other side, he faced another storm—the storm within this insane man possessed of demons. He had been driven from home and friends by the evil spirits. He lived among the tombs where night and day he cut himself with stones and cried out. When some tried to tie him up with chains, in demonic strength he broke loose. But when he saw Jesus, he ran to him and worshipped him.

Facing Jesus, the demons knew they would be cast out. Not wanting to leave that area, they asked permission to go into a herd of swine feeding nearby. Having left the man and entering into the swine, the insane man became normal, healed, delivered, and in his right mind.

As Jesus started to leave in the boat, the man asked if he could go with him. But Jesus said: "Go home to thy friends, and tell them how great things the Lord hath done for thee." HE WENT HOME ANOTHER WAY!

We can almost picture the scene. Not only children, but adults too, were afraid of him. Someone may have seen him coming and called out a warning to others who scurried away to hide from the mad man. But as he got closer, they would have seen he had his clothes on. The wild stare was gone. He was normal, in his right mind. It was the same road he had walked before, but now, now he was coming home ANOTHER WAY! He had met the Master. His life had been changed.

And there was the woman to whom Jesus spoke at Jacob's well (John 4:5-42). It was a laborious task to constantly go to a well in those days to obtain water.

126

When Jesus spoke of water that one could drink and "never thirst again," her response was this: "Sir, give me this water, that I thirst not, *neither come hither to draw.*" But Jesus spoke of *spiritual* water, a well of water within a person, "springing up into everlasting life."

She was surprised that Jesus even talked to her, since the Jews had no dealings with Samaritans. Nor was a Jewish religious teacher supposed to speak to any woman in a public place, according to the traditions of the time. Besides, she had been married five times and was now living with a man she was not married to! But Jesus looked beyond all of this and saw her need.

In the natural, it was still four months until the harvest, but here was a spiritual harvest to be reaped then and there. Here was a woman, no doubt a victim in many ways, who was thirsting for the water of life. Jesus revealed that God is not partial to some geographical location, whether Jerusalem or Samaria, but God "seeketh" worshippers on the basis of spirit and truth.

She believed that the Messiah was to come. When Jesus revealed himself to her as that very person, her life was transformed. In the joy and excitement of this grand revelation, she even forgot to take her waterpot with her, and headed home—now a messenger of the Messiah! "The woman then left her waterpot, and went her way into the city, and saith to the men, Come, see a man, which told me all things that ever I did: is not this the Christ?" Her life was changed; SHE WENT HOME ANOTHER WAY!

The man that we know as Paul, the apostle, was originally a fierce fighter of Christianity. While still "a young man" he took part in the stoning of Stephen and a "great persecution against the church which was at Jerusalem" (Acts 7:58, 8:1). He fanatically carried out his hatred for Christians, so that later he would say, "Beyond measure I persecuted the church of God, and wasted it" (Gal. 1:13). But one day, "breathing out threatenings and slaughter against the disciples of the Lord," as he neared Damascus, a great light shined around him and he heard the voice of Jesus Christ. His life was changed, transformed. He ended up on "Straight" Street (Acts 9:1-11). God takes people from Crooked Street and puts them on Straight Street! Paul WENT HOME ANOTHER WAY.

In the years that followed, God changed many other lives through the ministry of Paul. One convert was a jailer at Philippi (Acts 16:16-34). Having cast a spirit of divination out of a Philippi fortune teller, Paul and Silas were arrested and publicly humiliated in the town square. They were stripped of their clothing and beaten with many stripes. The jailor, being given strict orders regarding the imprisonment of these men, then "thrust them into the inner prison, and made their feet fast in the stocks."

But when they began to pray and praise at midnight, there was a massive earthquake, "and immediately all the doors were opened, and every one's bands were loosed." The jailor supposed the prisoners had fled, pulled out his sword, and was about to commit suicide in his desperation. We have included here an old drawing of the scene.

Paul cried out, assuring him they had not escaped. With this the jailor "came trembling, and fell down before Paul and Silas," and asked: "SIRS, what must I do to be saved?" Notice the change in attitude! This rough, tough, jailor—meaner than a junkyard dog—now calls them "Sirs"! He wants to know how to be saved!

That night Paul and Silas went to that man's house, he washed their stripes, was baptized, and served them supper! HE WENT HOME ANOTHER WAY! Later, Paul wrote the book of Philippians to this man, his family, and the church that developed there from these unique beginnings!

In the Old Testament, Samuel prophesied to Saul that the spirit of the Lord would come upon him and turn him *"into another man"* and give him *"another heart"* (1 Sam. 10:6, 9). With changes like these in his life, we can be sure that he WENT HOME ANOTHER WAY!

You see, God is a specialist in heart transplants. He promises: "A new heart also will I give you...I will take away the stony heart out of your flesh...ye shall be my people, and I will be your God" (Ezek. 36:26-28).

This concept of change is at the very heart of the gospel. It is called by such terms as: "newness of life" (Rom. 6:4), "born again" (John 1:13; 3:3), "converted" (Acts 3:19). Paul summed it up well in these words: "If any man be in Christ, he is a new creature: old things are passed away; behold, *all things are become new"* (2 Cor. 5:17).

Through Philip's ministry in Samaria, an entire city had been moved for God. But then, Philip was divinely directed to leave the crowds, to go talk to one man: a man he would find riding in a chariot on the desert road from Jerusalem to Gaza. This man, a government official from Ethiopia, had traveled all the way to Jerusalem—quite a trip in those days—to worship. He was now on his way home, but his life had not been changed.

He did have the book of Isaiah—which he may have purchased while in Jerusalem—and was reading from this book out loud. When Philip, having now run to catch up with the chariot, heard him read about one who was "led as a sheep to the slaughter," he called to him and asked if he understood. He did not; and invited Philip up into the chariot to explain. "Then Philip opened his mouth, and began at the same scripture, and preached unto him Jesus." (We have included here an artist's concept of the scene).

Philip's message apparently included water baptism, for as they rode along they came to water and the Ethiopian wanted to be baptized! Making certain that the man had believed in Jesus Christ with all his heart, he baptized him. Suddenly Philip disappeared, vanished into thin air, as it were. The Ethiopian looked around, but Philip was gone! Nevertheless, "he went on his way rejoicing" (Acts 8:27-40). HE WENT HOME ANOTHER WAY! His encounter with Jesus Christ changed his life.

In all of this we see God's plan. Philip left the crowds in Samaria to talk to one man who was, probably, a key man to reach many more. Having baptized this man, "the Spirit of the Lord caught away Philip" so that he was "found at Azotus" and completed a preaching circuit. He, too, WENT HOME ANOTHER WAY!

Over fifty years ago now, Oswald Smith penned these words of a hymn regarding the change that Jesus makes in lives:

> When Jesus comes the tempter's power is broken;
> When Jesus comes the tears are wiped away.
> He takes the gloom and fills the life with glory,
> For *all is changed* when Jesus comes to stay.

Another hymn expresses it in these words:

> What a wonderful *change* in my life has been wrought,
> Since Jesus came into my heart.

One man, having received Christ, sang it this way: "What a wonderful change in my *wife* has been wrought, since Jesus came into my heart!" When he got his own life in order, it seemed to him that even his wife had changed for the better! Some people continue to change jobs, change mates, and change friends—not recognizing that it is their *own lives* that need to be changed. It's easy to blame others, but consider this: "When a man's ways please the Lord, he maketh *even his enemies* to be at peace with him" (Pro. 16:7).

When people profess to be "saved," yet they are living in sin, just what, we ask, are they saved from? Christ came to save people *"from* their sins" (Matt. 1:21), not *in* their sins.

Some people say: "We all sin every day and need to repent every night!" But the Christian, whose life has been changed by Christ, does *not* habitually commit sin; he does *not* sin every day and need to repent every night! This would not be victorious living. How much better to start the day with a prayer: "Lord, I thank you for keeping me from sin. Thank you for victory today!"

The negative, defeated, idea that "we all sin every day" is not Bible doctrine. The Bible does not say, *"When we sin"*—as though we did it every day—but rather, "IF any man sin, we have an advocate with the Father, Jesus Christ." This is prefaced with these words: "My little children, these things write I unto you, that ye SIN NOT" (1 John 2:1).

"Oh, we are all just poor sinners," some say, "there is none righteous, no not one." But when the Bible says, "There is none righteous, no, not one" (Rom. 3:10), it is NOT talking about the born again believer! Look at the context. Those described do not understand, do not seek God, they do no good, their throat is an open sepulchre, deceit is on their tongues, the poison of asps is under their lips, their mouth is full of cursing and bitterness, they murder, they have not known the way of peace, and they do not fear God! This is not talking about the child of God! The point Paul is making is that neither the Jews as a people or Gentiles as a people are righteous (verse 9).

When the Bible says, "There is none righteous," it is evident he is not talking about those who are in Christ. "For he hath made him to be sin for us, who knew no sin; that we might be made the righteousness of God in him" (2 Cor. 5:21). Being cleansed "from all UNrighteousness" (1 John 1:9), believers are made "righteous" as numerous verses mention (James 5:16; 1 Peter 3:12).

All emphasis on church joining, doctrinal points, rules, regulations, and religious ceremonies—if lives are not changed—misses the mark. It is merely "having a form of godliness, but denying the power thereof" (2 Tim. 3:5). But

132

when we see a man changed from meanness to meekness—when God turns a big jug of honey over in his soul and sweetens up his disposition —this is real! When we see "old things pass away" —the alcoholism, the drug abuse, the cussing, the  hate, the lying, the cheating—and "all things become new"—he becomes a better father, a better husband, a better neighbor, a better citizen—this is exciting!

When we come together as Christians, we need prayer meetings with power. Theology can never take the place of kneeology. We need anointed preaching that will challenge and change. We need services in which God is glorified, the saints are edified, and Satan is horrified! Then it is that people will come to church and GO HOME ANOTHER WAY!

There are some who speak against giving an "altar call." They point out there is no specific examples in the ministry of Christ or the apostles where they asked people to "come forward." But before we are too quick to criticize the invitation system, we should face the fact that in this way—as well as other ways—people *have* come to the Lord in repentance and faith. I would not limit God. God may touch a man's life when he's driving down the road or out in the field plowing corn. The main thing is that men meet the Master; that their lives are changed; that they GO HOME ANOTHER WAY!

The wise men journeyed to Bethlehem. Since that time literally millions of people have also journeyed there on tours. Why? There is nothing spectacular about the scenery. It is no different than many other towns in that part of the world as far as its buildings, people, or geography. Why is this little town known world-wide, why do hymns include the name of this insignificant town? Its fame is for one reason only: *Jesus.*

Or consider Nazareth. Even at the time of Jesus, it was no great city. It was asked: "Can there any good thing come out of Nazareth?" (John 1:46). It was not the scene of any great revival or spiritual outpouring. Even with all the success Jesus had other places, of Nazareth it is written: "He could there do no mighty work" (Mark 6:5). Today, Nazareth has had a communist mayor, is still not the scene of revival, is not significant in any way, nor would tourists bother to go there, except for one thing: *Jesus!*

Jesus lived in Nazareth most of his life. Without last names as now, people were often associated with their home town, so that Jesus was known as Jesus *of Nazareth!* At his empty tomb, angels announced that Jesus of Nazareth was not there, but had risen! When the lame man, who was laid at the gate of the temple was healed, it was in the name of Jesus Christ of Nazareth! Even demons cried out: "Let us alone...thou Jesus of Nazareth"!

Because he was Jesus of Nazareth, sometimes early Christians were referred to as "the sect of the Nazarenes" (Acts 24:5). One of our Christian denominations today is called the Church of the Nazarene. Interesting that the name of a United States denomination would be based on a small town in a completely different part of the world!

The word "Calvary," which appears one time in the Bible (Lk. 23:33, KJV), means *skull.* It was a place where criminals were executed, a place of death. But "Calvary" has now taken on a new meaning, for it was here that Jesus died for us! It is not unusual for the word Calvary to be used in the names of churches such as Calvary Chapel, Calvary Bible Church, Calvary Temple, or Calvary Assembly. Had it not been for the difference that Jesus makes, to use such names would be like calling a church The Skull Church!

The cross itself was an instrument of execution and death. To preach a message of *life,* and link it with an instrument of *death,* as Paul admitted, was "foolishness" to the unconverted, "but unto us which are saved it is the power of God" (1 Cor. 1:18). Execution by death on a cross was common in the first century. Compare this with a modern form of execution: the electric chair. Imagine instead of singing, "There's room at the cross for you," we might sing: "There's room at the electric chair for you"! Instead of singing "At the cross, at the cross, where I first saw the light," we might sing, "At the electric chair, at the electric chair, where I first saw the light"! What makes the difference? *Jesus Christ.*

All of these things are changed because of *Him.* He takes the BAD and makes it BEAUTIFUL. He takes us from the mire to the choir! He takes our sin and gives salvation. He turns vice to victory, bondage to blessing, and replaces doubts with shouts! He gives us a clean slate.

And so, I must ask each of you who will read these words: Have YOU made peace with God through Him who said: "I am the way, the truth, and the life, no man cometh unto the Father but by me" (Jn. 14:6)? Have you received Jesus Christ as *your* Lord and Savior? Have you followed Him in water baptism; have you received his Holy Spirit into your life? Have you experienced his love whereby you can *know* you have passed from death to life? Have you been changed so that old things have passed away and all things have become *new?* By his transforming grace, YOU can experience TRIUMPH OUT OF TRAGEDY and GO HOME ANOTHER WAY!

The Bridge Builder

An old man traveling a lone highway
Came in the evening cold and gray
To a chasm deep and wide.
The old man crossed in the twilight dim,
The sullen stream had no fears for him,
But he stopped when safe on the other side
And built a bridge to span the tide.

"Old man," said a fellow pilgrim near,
"You're wasting your strength with building here;
Your journey will end with the ending day,
You never again will pass this way,
You've crossed the chasm deep and wide,
Why build you this bridge at eventide?"

The builder lifted his old gray head,
"Good friend, in the path I've come," he said,
"There followeth after me today
A youth whose feet must pass this way.
This chasm which has been as naught to me
To that fair-haired youth might a pitfall be,
He, too, must cross in the twilight dim,
Good friend, I am building this bridge for him."

—Will Allen Dromgoole